Unlock the Power of your Credit Score

notionpress.com

Unlock the Power of your Credit Score

Arun Ramamurthy
Gaurav Wadhwani
Aman Kapoor

notionpress.com

Notion Press

Old No. 38, New No. 6,

McNichols Road, Chetpet,

Chennai - 600 031

First Published by Notion Press 2015

ISBN: 978-93-5206-298-0

Foreword

Your Credit Score is really important. From the big decisions to the little ones that you take every day, a lot hinges on this three digit number. The lack of awareness of credit scores has meant that many people are not aware of its significance in their lives.

The authors are known to me by virtue of the work that they do in their business. When I heard that they were writing a book on the subject, I was happy to see that there would, at last, be an attempt to "demystify" the credit score, and provide people with practical tools to manage their credit and benefit from it.

This book is very informative and tells you how one can lead a credit healthy life. It is lucidly written, and is not riddled with the business jargon that one usually finds in such books. The book is a must-read for anyone who has availed of credit facilities or plans to avail of them in the future. It will be a tremendous help to guiding you on managing your finances for a healthy credit life.

Nanoo Pamnani
Director, Bajaj Finance;
Vice Chairman, Bajaj Finserv;
Former Chief Executive Officer, Citibank, N.A., India

Need For the Book

Now a man is like this or like that,
According as he acts and according as he behaves, so will he be.
A man of good acts will become good; a man of bad acts, bad;
He becomes pure by pure deeds, bad by bad deeds.

Brihadranyaka Upanishad
(Verse 4.4.5-6)

Credit is an integral part of every adult Indian's financial life. Access to credit is increasingly a function of our past actions which are evaluated in statistical terms such as credit scores. More than 20 crore people in India have a credit score. However, only a miniscule percentage knows its true importance. The karmic significance of our credit actions gives the authors hope that we can all do better, when armed with the knowledge of how credit scores work. This hope is the driving force behind this book and is an attempt to help people to "discover" the "Credit Score" and guide them on how they can harness its true potential.

Introduction

India is a young country with about 65% of the population under the age of 35* years. With a median age of 25 years, more and more people continue to get inducted into the workforce every year. This is expected to result in an astronomical increase in the demand for all kinds of products and services, in turn fueling the demand for credit.

Retail credit penetration in India is far lower than even smaller countries such as Thailand and Vietnam. This combined with India's young population is indicative of the growth potential for credit products in the near future.

The importance of retail credit in our lives underlines the need for everyone to be credit healthy. A good understanding of credit and its active management could prove to be the key to a world of conveniences and opportunities. However, a lack of understanding on how to manage credit can lead to a situation that potentially could be financially devastating. It is equally true that the awareness of credit and credit management tools is very low among the general population in India.

This book is a humble attempt to inculcate greater awareness about the concept of being credit healthy among people. It has been our endeavor to explain basic credit concepts in a simple yet effective fashion that can appeal to a wider audience. Additionally, we have tried to add illustrations and graphs wherever possible so as to make the content more interesting.

We wish that this book provides people with insights into the basics of credit and its active management which could prove to be the key to a hidden fortune.

---

* Source: India Census Survey: 2011

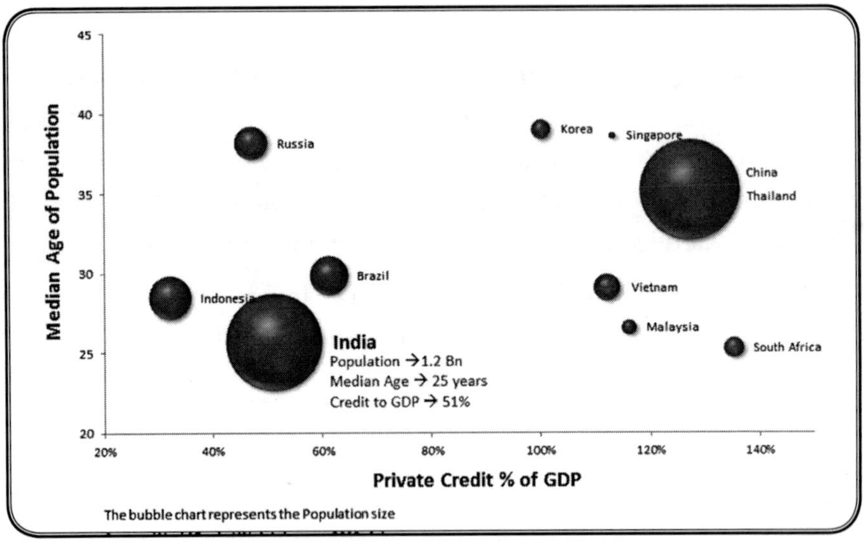

India: Demographics Led Surge for Retail Credit

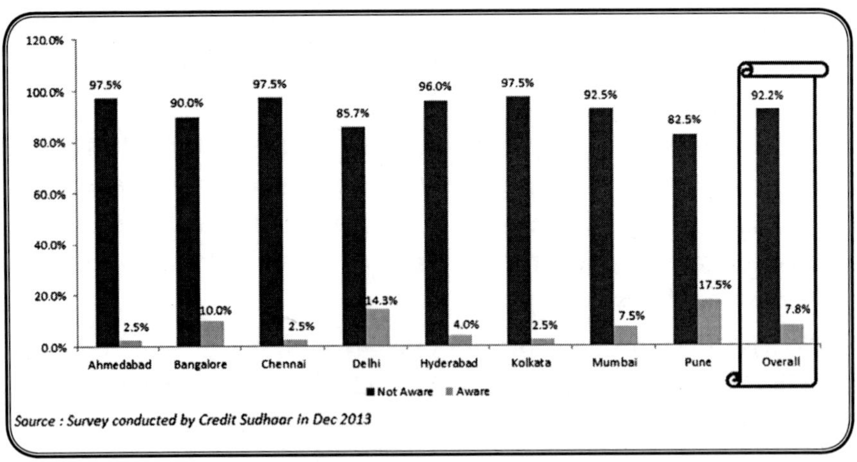

Awareness of Credit Reports and Scores in India

Contents

PART I

Building Blocks of Credit

Originating in the 1530s, the word "Credit" is said to have its roots in Old Italian, *Credito,* or Latin, *Creditum*. The word has the following meanings:

- A source of pride or honor (*source of credit to your family/society/school/nation*)
- Honor given for some action (*For example, "staff was given due credit for its bravery"*)
- Trustworthiness (*For example, "witness in court shall be of credit"*)
- Confidence in a purchaser's or borrower's ability to pay/repay

It is evident from the above meanings that the word is intimately associated with one's PRIDE. Whether it is about being honored for a task or being held trustworthy for our actions or managing our finances, it is our reputation and faith that control our social, emotional and financial wellbeing.

The link between credit and money is based on these very concepts of credibility and dependability. Money is often perceived as a yardstick for success and the money that a person can raise or borrow depends on one's credibility in the market.

While the origin of the term "credit" can be traced back to about 500 years, lending and borrowing has possibly existed since the beginning of humanity. As civilizations developed and money markets evolved, the process of lending and borrowing has also advanced.

Before we get to understand today's evolved lending process, let us evaluate the following situations.

Situation 1

You are approached by an office colleague whom you know for the last 3 years. He is your peer in office and has a habit of asking for loans. While in the past he has returned the money he borrowed, but over the last few occasions, he has not been prompt and has required reminders.

Situation 2

You are approached by a colleague whom you know for the last one month. He is your peer in office and has a designation similar to you. He approaches you with a request for some money with a commitment to return it in a week's time.

Situation 3

You are approached by a colleague who works as an office clerk with a request to lend him Rs. 5,000 which he promises to return on his pay day. The clerk also tells you that he has been asked to get in touch with you by his supervisor who is out of office and hence is not able to help him with money. You speak to his supervisor (who also happens to be your friend) to confirm the details. Your friend endorses the request.

What is the likely outcome of each of the above situations? Whom would you lend your money to?

Situation 1

You cannot be sure if you will be able to get your money back, given your colleague's recent track record. Hence, the likelihood of lending the money is low.

Situation 2

You do not know the person well enough and may not be willing to risk your hard earned money.

Situation 3

While the office clerk is relatively unknown to you, you might still be motivated to lend the money to him, given that the risk is mitigated by an assurance from his supervisor who is known to you.

As seen in above situations, it was fairly intuitive to decide on the requests based on the information available to make these decisions.

A lending institution faces similar and more complex challenges. Lending is the core of its business model (Risk and Reward go hand in hand for any lending institution). The lending institution often has little or no information about the risk posed by an individual applicant. This makes the decision making process much more involved and specialized.

How does the lender then arrive at a decision?

Borrowing and lending are possibly among the oldest professions on earth. The legal framework for credit dates back to 1800 BC when Hammurabi, the King of the first dynasty of Babylon, authored the earliest known formal laws. In these laws, we find the first recorded attempt to regulate interest rates. Hammurabi established a ceiling or maximum rate of interest that a moneylender could charge a borrower.

Credit Underwriting

Credit underwriting can be defined as "a process that assists the lender to take prudent decisions on whether or not to extend a credit facility on a borrower's request while taking into account all risk factors".

From a risk assessment perspective, an underwriter assesses a loan application in the light of three broad parameters. These parameters are called the **3Cs of Credit:**

C
apacity
haracter
ollateral.

Case Study

Assume you are working in a mid-sized company as an executive. Arjun Kumar is a middle aged colleague who shares the same designation as you in the organization. He has been working in the company for five years and has a salary of Rs. 50,000 per month. Arjun approaches you with a request to lend him Rs. 20,000. Please evaluate this request in the light of the following three situations:

Situation 1

- Arjun has approached you for a loan prior to this occasion as well and has repaid the loan promptly.
- Arjun has been struggling professionally over the last few months and is perceived to be underachiever. You have also heard from the grapevine that Arjun may soon be terminated for poor job performance.

Situation 2

- Arjun has never approached you for a loan prior to this occasion.
- You know that Arjun has a few active loans from banks but over the last few months, the banks' collectors have been visiting Arjun's office to meet him.

Situation 3

- You know that Arjun has been in the habit of taking loans from you. He has been regular in paying back these loans. But this time, the amount is much larger than on the previous occasions.
- While requesting for the loan, Arjun is ready to hand over his watch (the price of which is far more than the value of the loan) to you with a promise to pay the loan back in a month (and take his watch back).
    - What shall be your lending decision in each of the above situations?
    - What would be the considerations while arriving at a decision?

Possible response to situation 1

You may not lend money despite that fact that Arjun is known to you for 5 years and earns a good salary because the continuity of his income is doubtful (considering the probability of Arjun losing his job)

Possible response to situation 2

You may not lend money to Arjun despite knowing him for five years and him earning a good salary since his current financial condition is under question. The fact that he is being approached by collection agencies raises questions about his repayment track record.

Possible response to situation 3

Arjun is known to you for 5 years and has a stable job. While he has requested you for an amount which is higher than before, you may still lend him the money since he is ready to keep his watch with you (the fact that the value of watch is far higher than the loan amount, gives you additional comfort)

***In India, Kautilya's Arthashastra (400 BC) gives detailed references regarding the rates of interest that maybe charged by money lenders to different types of borrowers. Five **panas per cent per month was commercial interest (Vyavahariki). Ten panas per month per cent was for ventures that crossed forests. Twenty panas per month per month prevailed among sea traders (Samudramam). The riskier the nature of the business, the higher the rate of interest.**

Let us now have a look at the three important pillars of underwriting (the 3Cs of Credit) in the context of the above mentioned situations.

* *(R Sharmashastry, Government Press, Bangalore, 1915 - The Arthashastra of Kautilya)*

** *Pana: Coinage minted in India around 600 BC. The Pana had four denominations; One Pana, Half Pana (Ardhapana), Quarter Pana (Pada) and One Eighth Pana (Ashtha-bhaga or Arshapadika)*

3 Cs of Credit Framework – Capacity, Collateral and Character

As mentioned earlier, credit underwriting can be defined as a process which evaluates a loan application on three parameters; namely the 3Cs of credit.

C1 : Capacity

C2 : Character

C3 : Collateral

Capacity and character form the prerequisites of any loan application. In the absence of any of these parameters, a loan application has a high chance of rejection.

C1 – Capacity

Credit Capacity or the capability to repay the loan amount is the first step for a loan application to get reviewed favorably. In case the applicant does not have the required income levels, the lending institution may reject the application or review it for a lower amount which the underwriter feels is within the borrower's repayment means.

C2 – Character

Credit Character can be defined as the willingness or intentions of an individual to repay a loan. Even if the borrower has the requisite income levels and is in a position to repay, the slightest doubt on his intentions could cause the underwriter to reject the loan request. The assessment of an applicant's credit character is probably the most important step in the credit evaluation process.

C3 – Collateral

An asset pledged with a lending institution against a loan is called Collateral.

A loan secured by Collateral (called secured lending) carries a lower risk than one without Collateral (called unsecured lending). Once the repayment Capacity and Credit Character is ascertained, a loan application is reviewed in the light of the 3rd C (Collateral)

Generally, in the case of a loan application secured against Collateral, the chances of approval are likely to be higher than in the case of an unsecured loan.

Arjun	C1 Capacity	C2 Character	C3 Collateral
Situation 1	✗	✓	Not Available
Situation 2	?	✗	Not Available
Situation 3	?	✓	✓

Review of Arjun's request using the 3C framework

Situation 1

Arjun does not qualify on Capacity (C1) while he has good Credit Character (C2). His capacity to repay is under question given that he may lose his job in the near future.

Situation 2

Arjun's Credit Capacity (C1) is questionable. However, he clearly disqualifies on Credit Character (C2). He has perhaps been defaulting on loans recently.

Situation 3

Arjun's Credit Capacity (C1) is perhaps stretched but he has repaid loans in the past. Also, the loan is secured against Collateral (C3).

Credit Capacity

Assessing Credit Capacity, as we learn in detail a little later, is actually a mathematical calculation based on the income and expense of an individual. On the face of it, it seems to be a fairly simple task to calculate this based on all the earnings and all the expenditures of an individual. Given the ground realities in the Indian context, it often turns out to be a highly complex job. Poor accounting and reporting standards, a large cash economy along with gross under-reporting of incomes and inflation of expenses make it difficult for an underwriter to assess an applicant's Credit Capacity (especially in the non-salaried segment)

Credit Capacity is measured at two levels. At the first level it is evaluated at "current" levels of income and expense. At the second level, it is measured in terms of "stability" of such incomes over a period of time. Both these evaluations are essential to ensure that the loan repayment sustains over its designated tenure.

Current Income

The capacity to repay can be ascertained from the documents provided by the borrower.

$$\text{Debt Burden Ratio} = \frac{\text{Monthly outflow on all credit facilities}}{\text{Net Monthly Income}}$$

Underwriters commonly use a ratio called the "Debt to Burden Ratio" (DBR) to evaluate an applicant's current capacity to repay. Mathematically speaking, the DBR is the ratio of total monthly obligations to total monthly income. As a prudential norm, 50% of an individual's income is considered to be a "safe" debt burden ratio. This implies that the applicant can avail a loan to the extent where his monthly obligations (EMIs) are not more than half of his monthly income.

Vikramjeet has a net salary of Rs. 73,000 and is servicing three loans including one auto loan, one personal loan and one consumer durable loan with EMIs of Rs. 14,500, Rs. 11,000 and Rs. 1,750 respectively. The total obligation on the EMIs amounts to Rs. 27,250 which is 37% of Vikramjeet's salary. Thus, his current DBR is 37% and he has an available DBR limit of 13% (assuming that the acceptable DBR is set at 50 %)

In the case of a salaried applicant, the pay slip (which reflects the applicant's income) and the bank statement help to define the Credit Capacity. Salary credits, bank account balances, cheque bounces, regular debits of similar amounts and other such factors help in the interpretation of repayment capacity.

However, this is not the same in case of a self-employed applicant. In this segment, the declared income (as declared in the income tax returns) is often lower than the actual income in a large proportion of the cases. The bank account transactions (as in the case of a salaried applicant) may not be a true measure of the applicant's income and expense. This makes the calculation of an individual's actual DBR a difficult task in the case of the self-employed segment.

The underwriter is primarily bound to take the declared income into account to calculate DBR. In certain cases, the business profile may also influence the outcome of the loan request (especially in the case of a loan being applied in the name of a business entity – called business loan). Factors such as business turnover, available stocks and receivables may also get factored in the underwriting process.

"Stability" of Income

Income flows could be prone to high volatility in today's globalized environment. Businesses often get impacted by events that occur many thousands of miles away. The 2007 subprime crisis had a cascading effect on the global economy. Consequently, several Indian sectors including airlines, hotels, real estate, exports, IT & BPO industries among others, were severely impacted. This led to both business and job losses.

Given that a loan needs to be serviced over its entire tenure, establishing stability or continuity of income is very important. The following are some of the factors that help to determine "stability of income".

Salaried Segment

- The organization a person is employed with (multinational or domestic; public limited or privately held company; line of business)
- The seniority of the person in the organization
- The duration of employment of the person with the same organization
- The total work experience of the person across his career

Self-employed segment

- Educational qualification
- Entity status (partnership, proprietorship or private limited company)
- Length of business operations
- Type/ profilc of business
- Gross turnover
- Cash flows in the bank statement

All of the above, when viewed in totality, give an indication about the sustainability of future earnings. This helps the underwriter to decide the next course of action on the credit application.

The first Credit Card was issued in 1949 by a company called Diners Club International. By 1951, there were over 20,000 Diners Club cardholders.

In 2012, there were around 883.5 million Visa credit cards in circulation worldwide while the number of MasterCard credit cards in circulation worldwide amounted to 721.4 million cards*

---

* *http://www.statista.com/statistics/279257/number-of-credit-cards-in-circulation-worldwide. MasterCard and Visa are two of the most popular credit card networks in the world.*

Collateral

Collateral can be defined as an asset pledged with the lender as a security against a loan. In the event of default, the lender has the right to dispose off the collateral to recover the outstanding amount and the loss/expenses (if any).

Firming up the value of Collateral is a tedious task as the underwriter needs to factor in various aspects like the current valuation of property, expected price fluctuations over time, and external factors which can lead to the market behaving adversely (this could even be on account of natural calamities and various domestic or international events beyond one's immediate control)

Uncommon Forms of Collateral

- The Italian regional bank, Credito Emiliano, accepts cheese (Parmigiano-Reggiano) as collateral, and then ages it in climate-controlled vaults.
- Intellectual property (trademarks, patents), Insurance policies are also other forms of uncommon collateral.
- In 2011, there was widespread anger in Greece over the terms being discussed by creditor nations (which included Germany and France). These nations were suggesting that they might demand a mortgage over Greece's historic antiquities – or even a lien over some of the country's Aegean islands to secure bailout loans to the island nation.

Various types of collaterals are accepted by lending institutions. Following is a list of collaterals accepted by lenders for different types of loans.

- Real Estate (home loan, loan against property)
- Gold (loan against gold)
- Vehicle (auto loan)
- Stocks/Bonds/Mutual Funds (loan against shares)

Credit Character

In general, Credit Character forms the basis of the confidence a lender would have in the borrower to repay a loan as per agreed terms.

Credit Character involves assessing a person's performance on credit facilities and how one approaches his responsibilities towards debtors during good and bad times.

Till about 2006, due to the inadequate presence of credit bureaus in India, lending institutions were relying upon information collected through informal sources such as verification agencies. The information furnished by these agencies was subjective since the verifiers would draw inferences from what they saw or heard (from neighbors and friends among others).

As observed in Arjun's example (situation 2), his Credit Character was in doubt given his poor repayment history. Judging a borrower's Credit Character is the foundation of most underwriting decisions all over the world.

How is Credit Character Measured?

Measuring any individual's character is a subjective matter and prone to bias and interpretation. Assessing Credit Character, in this context, is even more complex given the stakes involved in any lending decision.

In theory, an underwriter could determine Credit Character based on the following four methods:

1. Personal interaction to assess a borrower's Credit Character
2. Internal database checks
3. Benchmarking the applicant (based on past lending experiences) against performance of peer group/ age group/ geography and other factors

The Great Indian Retail Meltdown Of 2008

- In 2007, the United States, the European Union and Japan were affected by a deep recession that was triggered by the collapse of the subprime mortgage market in the USA.
- Related only in part to the above crisis, the retail unsecured lending market (credit cards and personal loans) in India collapsed.
- Till 2006, lending institutions were underwriting loans in a non-bureau framework. This led to overleveraged clients, who ultimately defaulted on their loans.
- Over leveraging and a weak economy meant that unsecured portfolio loss rates were as high as 40% in some lending institutions.
- To illustrate the situation, in 2008, India had 27.50 crore credit cards in circulation which dropped to 18 crore in 2010. The high loss rates caused banks to restructure their customer base. Thousands of credit cards were cancelled. Even today, India has only about 21 crore credit cards in circulation.

- **The secured loan (Housing loans and loans against property) portfolios remained largely unaffected by this downturn.**
- **This meltdown heralded the beginning of several reforms in credit underwriting in India, including the extensive use of credit bureaus by lending institutions.**

4. Assessment of all relevant facts pertaining to an applicant's record on all previous loans and any other credit relationship with any lending institution

Decision Factor	Description	Data Availability For Inference	Quality Of Data For Inference	Subjectivity In Decision Making	Credit Decision
Personal interaction	Driven by the individual	Limited	Low	High	Prone to errors
Drawing upon internal data	Limited to internal base	Limited	High	Medium	Prone to errors
Benchmarking inferences	Benchmarking against peer group/ age group/ residential group	Limited	High	Medium	Prone to errors
Factual data from reliable sources	Based on authentic facts and figures	High	High	Low	Proficient

Decision Methods to measure Credit Character

Needless to say, a decision process where data quality (in terms of accuracy and relevance) is high, where data quantity is abundant and the decision mechanism is objective; is ideal for effective decision making.

It is in this context that Credit Bureaus play a critical role.

Definition of a Credit Bureau

A Credit Bureau is a data repository that receives and maintains data of individuals and entities for the purpose of reporting to either the approved institutions or to individuals

Credit Bureau – A True Measure of Credit Character

A Credit Bureau is a data repository that receives and maintains data of individuals and entities. It not only collects the data from lending institutions but also enhances its quality by presenting historical credit behavior and analytics for the purpose of taking prudent and informed lending decisions.

The information and analytics that is made available to underwriters from the credit bureaus is high on quantity (since it captures details on all the loan accounts of an individual) and on quality (given the regular updation of the current status of every credit account by lending institutions). This helps underwriters to assess the risk associated with an applicant.

About Credit Bureaus

The history of organized credit bureaus dates back to 1898. It was then that Equifax (called "Retail Credit Company" at that time) was established in the USA by two brothers. What started off as an endeavor to create a list of customers with an indication of their credit worthiness for the local Retail Grocers' Association, has today turned into a multi-billion dollar global industry.

Nowadays, credit ratings have become an integral part of the global retail financial industry. As per World Bank* records, credit rating agencies are present in 102 countries capturing data on the adult population in varying degrees (depending on credit penetration). There are 23 countries where credit bureaus capture data on 100% of the adult population.

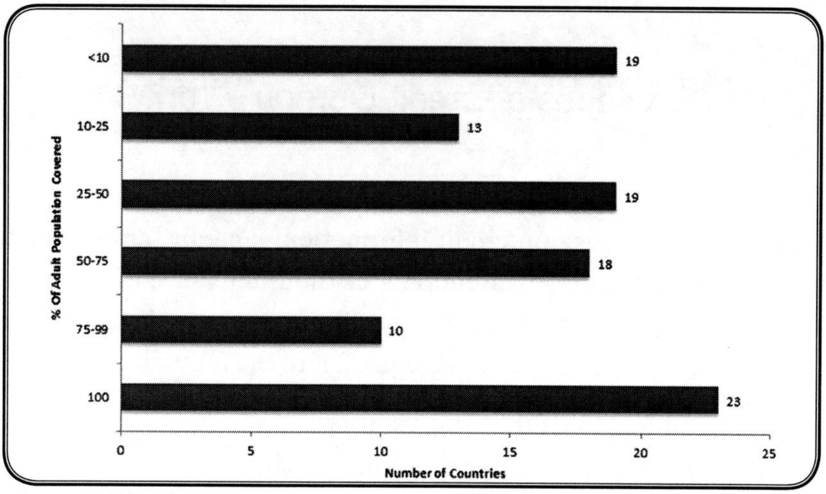

*Source: World bank**

Credit Bureau Coverage of the Adult Population

There are credit bureaus with a multinational presence and there are those which are indigenous and are present in a particular country only. The top three credit bureaus that have a multinational presence are:

- Equifax; established in 1898 at Atlanta, USA
- TransUnion; established in 1968 at Chicago, USA
- Experian; established in 1996 at Dublin, Ireland

In 1803, a group of English tailors got together to form the Mutual Communication Society of London. Its members had realized that some people purchased goods regularly from them and did not make good on their payments. This cooperative venture which was formed was perhaps the first credit information exchange in the world.

---

* *Source: http://data.worldbank.org/indicator/IC.CRD.PRVT.ZS/countries*

How does a Credit Bureau Work?

Being a data warehouse on credit information, a credit bureau collects data on the credit habits of hundreds of thousands of consumers and analyzes their data to assess the risk profile associated with a borrower. The working of a bureau can be segregated into the following categories:

1. Aggregate data from various sources
2. Map data correctly to individuals as required
3. Synthesize and analyze the large amounts of data which is available with them
4. Provide data and analytics to institutions and individuals based on prevailing norms

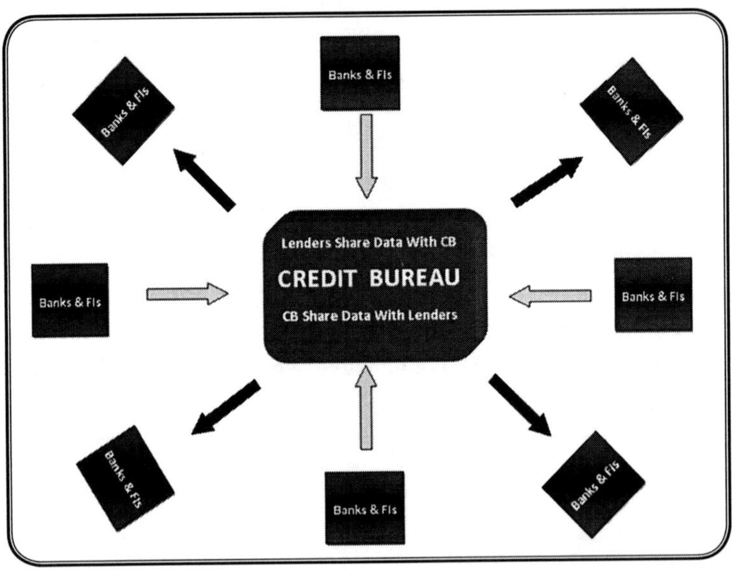

Credit Bureau – A Data Warehouse

As we see in the above illustration, the credit bureau collects data from and disseminates data to financial institutions. As a data repository

How Does a Credit Bureau earn Money?

- Credit Services

  This is the core offering of any credit bureau. Credit bureaus collate and sell details on all credit accounts availed by the consumer along with all required details based on a specific request from a lending institution. This helps the lending institution to take prudent decisions on a borrower's loan application.

- Decision Analytics:

  Analyzing the risk associated on different products or services for an individual and selling it along with the credit history is another source of revenue generation for the bureaus. The lending institutions pay a higher amount for such analysis as compared to buying just a report.

- Marketing Services:

  Lending institutions seek to provide credit facilities to creditworthy individuals. Recognizing this need, the bureaus offer services which help to screen the institution's customer database proactively (on pre-defined parameters) and share it with lending institutions (only in the case of a specific request from a LI). These customers (based on their past performance and other factors) might qualify for credit facilities. These offers are called "pre-approved offers".

- Consumer Services:

  In developed countries, credit bureaus also earn money by providing the report and analysis directly to the consumer. Apart from this, the bureaus have started offering additional services like credit monitoring and identity theft insurance to customers. This is the fastest growing revenue stream for the bureaus worldwide and accounts for a substantial proportion of the overall revenue of a credit bureau in developed economies.

(Database warehouse), a bureau is required to collate historical data pertaining to an individual or entity. This large database is then run through complex analytical algorithms (calculations) so that the data is available for users in a comprehensive yet usable format.

This data repository presents the historical data in a simple and easy to understand format to the users. It also analyzes data pertaining to an individual based on various parameters and hundreds of thousands of other individuals' data available with them.

Consumers' data captured by a credit bureau can be categorized into three segments.

1. Personal Details
2. Credit Account Details
3. Inquiries

The lending institutions submit updated data every month to all the credit bureaus. This not only helps in keeping the status of the credit accounts updated with the bureaus, but also facilitates accurate analysis of the credit risk posed by an applicant. This analysis helps the lending institutions to take informed underwriting decisions pertaining to a person's Credit Character.*

---

* *The Reserve Bank of India makes it mandatory for lending institutions to report data every month to all the credit bureaus.*

Credit Bureaus in India

India's first credit bureau, CIBIL (Credit Information Bureau of India) was established in August 2000. However, it was not until 2005 that the Credit Information Companies Act was passed as a law by an Act of Parliament.

While the Act is explained in detail in an annexure, it is important to know that today we have several credit bureaus in India. The four retail credit bureaus in India are:

CIBIL TransUnion	:	Established in Aug 2000 (Collaboration)
Experian	:	Established in Feb 2010 (Multinational)
Equifax	:	Established in Mar 2010 (Multinational)
Crif Highmark	:	Established in Nov 2010 (Collaboration)

Ever since their establishment, credit bureaus in India have grown both in terms of their size and importance. Today, it is estimated that credit bureaus in India store data for over 28, 00, 00,000 (28 crore) individuals comprising more than 52, 00, 00,000 (52 crore) loan/credit accounts.

With data of 28 crore people available with the credit bureaus, India has among the largest credit bureau databases in the world. The CIC (Credit Information Act of India) mandates all lending institutions to contribute consumer credit data at least once a month to every credit bureau in India

---

Growing impact of Credit Bureaus in India

In developed economies, credit bureaus have a far reaching impact on several facets of life. They contribute not only towards the lending decisions by a creditor, but also impact job offers, house renting decisions, insurance premiums, cost of telecom connections and other utilities among several aspects of life.

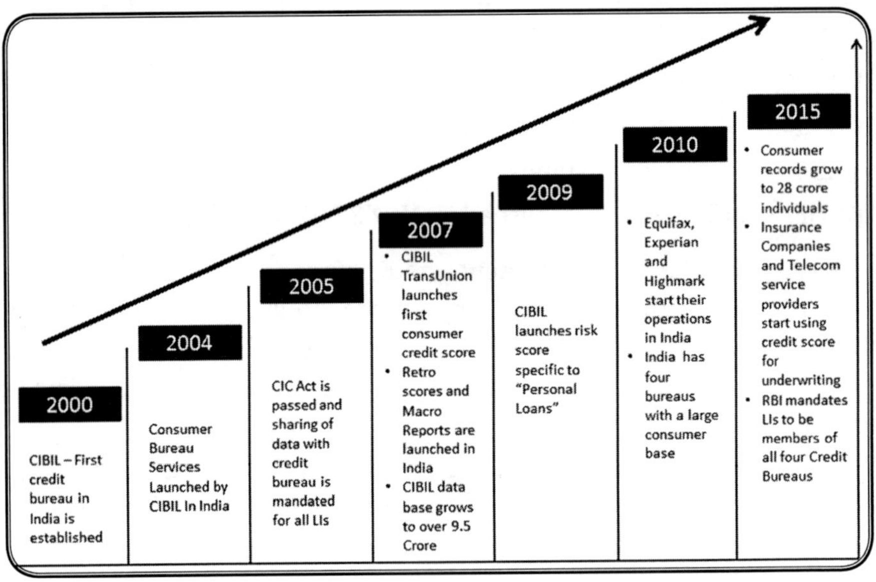

Growth of Credit Bureaus in India

Thus far in India, the credit bureaus primarily influence a loan decision. In the near future, the data in a bureau is expected to have a bearing on several other facets of our lives such as insurance, telecom and employment among others, just as it does in developed economies.

MCNF – MasterCard Negative File

In India, prior to credit bureaus, the "Satyam" database, also known as MCNF database (Master Card Negative File) was widely used in the market. The MCNF database is the database of all customers who have defaulted on their MasterCard credit card. The customer could belong to any bank which issues MasterCard credit cards. The Satyam database was widely used till about 2004, when with the advent of Credit Bureaus, it gradually diminished in importance.

Key Points

- Credit is an integral part of our day to day lives
- Being credit healthy is essential for one's financial wellbeing
- Credit assessment is a complex process and is based on the 3Cs of Credit:
    - Capacity
    - Character
    - Collateral
- Credit Character (credibility) of an applicant is a pre-eminent factor in the evaluation process of any credit application
- Credit Bureaus provide the best objective assessment of a person's Credit Character
- The Credit Information Act of 2005 paved the way for the operationalization of Credit Bureaus in India
- India has 4 retail Credit Bureaus: CIBIL, Equifax, Experian and Highmark
- Credit Bureau data coverage in India is increasing rapidly every year
- Credit Bureau data is being increasingly used in India for non-lending decisions (as is the case in other countries)

PART II

Credit Scores and their Importance

Deb Bhattacharya

Deb Bhattacharya works with a multinational company in Kolkata and earns Rs. 1, 05,000 a month. He is servicing a car loan apart from having five credit cards. An engineer and management graduate by qualification, Deb has been working for the last 3 years. He is unmarried and with his father being well placed, he has all his income at his disposal.

Deb wants to take his parents on a trip to Europe and decides to take a loan to fund his holiday. He applies for a personal loan.

Rashmi Bhansali

Rashmi earns a monthly salary of Rs. 60,000. Having lost her father in her childhood, she was brought up by her mother under economically challenging circumstances. A middle class upbringing has taught her the importance of money. She lives a simple life and has vowed not to take any loan as far as possible. She spends in cash and does not even have a credit card. Rashmi lives well within her means and parks all her savings in the form of fixed deposits with banks.

Her younger brother Rahul is a bright student and is in the final year of his engineering. He has also earned a scholarship for a year's course in a European university. Admission to this course would hone his skills and add to his resume. However, the scholarship is restricted to the course fees and Rahul is expected to manage the travel, visa, boarding and lodging costs by himself. The total cost amounts to around Rs. 6, 50,000. To help her brother, Rashmi decides to withdraw her bank fixed deposit of Rs. 1, 50,000 while hoping that the remaining amount can be funded through an education loan.

Prashant Ramaswamy

3 years ago, Prashant went through a difficult time with his business and lost a lot of money. At that time, a number of creditors, including banks, were knocking at his doors regularly to collect their money. Prashant sold the house that he had bought from his earnings to pay off his loans. Since the outstanding on his loans was higher than the selling price of the property, he had to settle a few bank loans.

Prashant was relieved that he had managed to get the creditors off his back. He is satisfied that his peer group appreciated his efforts and held him in high regard even though he had to sell his property.

After the struggle and hard work of the last 3 years, Prashant's business started to expand. He decided to apply for a business loan so that he could expand his operations.

Deb, Rashmi and Prashant are all planning to take loans to fulfill their needs.

What is the likely outcome of each of the above situations and their funding requests? What factors would the underwriter base these decisions on?

Let us look at the likely fate of their loan applications in the light of the first 2 Cs of the credit decision-making process (Credit Capacity and Credit Character)

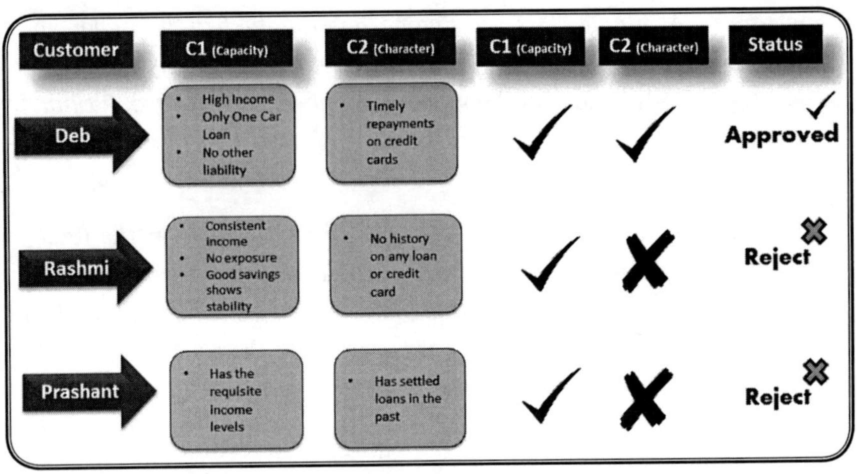

Loan Evaluation: Credit Capacity & Credit Character

Deb Bhattacharya has the requisite income levels and had repaid all his loan obligations on time in past. The lending institution had no hesitation in sanctioning a loan to Deb.

Rashmi Bhansali also has the requisite income levels to service the loan (perhaps she would have turned out to be a good repayment risk). However, in the absence of any credit history she is like a complete stranger to the lending institution. Rashmi had never taken a credit facility and not having any credit history means lack of information to assess her Credit Character. Not having any credit information is taken as a negative trait and works to Rashmi's disadvantage.

Prashant Ramaswamy also has the ability to service the loan, but has entered into settlements in the past and an underwriter would be weary of extending credit to a person who has borrowed money in the past and has caused losses to the lender.

In the case of Prashant, there could be a query as to why someone, who displayed strength of character by repaying his loan through the proceeds of his house, should be declined on a loan application. From an underwriting perspective, Prashant has not repaid in full. He settled his loans and the lenders lost money on credit facilities extended to him. This casts a shadow on Prashant's Credit Character: the likely assumption is that future loan disbursals may have the same outcome (settlement) as had happened earlier.

In all of the above case studies, the subjects had the requisite levels of income to service their loan requests. However, their past repayment track records decide their future capacity to avail credit facilities.

Where Deb scored while Prashant and Rashmi failed was on the important aspect of Credit Character. How does an underwriter obtain information on a borrowers' Credit Character?

An underwriter gets information on an individual's Credit Character from the credit bureau, in the form of a credit report.

What is a Credit Report?

A credit report is a comprehensive chronicle of an individual's credit history. Credit Reports are generated by credit bureaus. Credit bureaus use the large amounts of data (on various credit facilities) available with them to generate these reports.

A credit report has two primary objectives:

- To capture and collate all details pertaining to an individual's credit accounts
- To generate a score based on the account details

Every credit bureau in India has its own version of the credit report. Each of these reports has similar information. However, the format and presentation of the credit reports may be different for each of these bureaus

---

A typical credit bureau report consists of four sections:

1. Credit Score

   The credit score represents the credit worthiness of an individual and is the statistical outcome of the interaction of several parameters. It takes into account the historical data of the individual and the knowledge acquired through extensive analysis of the data available with the credit bureau.

2. Personal Details

   - Name/ DOB/ Gender
   - All addresses that have been reported by an individual (office and residence).
   - All contact numbers (mobile and landline).
   - Email IDs
   - All Government identity details that have been furnished to banks/ financial institutions

3. Account Details
    - Bank/Lender's Name
    - Type of loan
    - Account Number
    - Loan Amount
    - Interest Rate
    - Current Balance
    - Start Date
    - Close Date (if already closed)
    - Current Status (Open/Closed/Written Off/Settled among others)
    - Repayment history for the last 36 months
4. Inquiries
    - List of all banks/ lending institutions requesting for data on an individual
    - Product inquired for (such as personal loan, credit card, home loans and other credit facilities)
    - Amount applied for

What is a Credit Score?

A Credit Score is a three digit number that denotes an individual's creditworthiness. In other words, the credit score is a numerical measure of an individual's Credit Character.*

In India, the credit score is colloquially referred to as the "CIBIL score". The term "CIBIL score" has almost become synonymous with credit scores. Even so, it must be noted that credit scores from any of the bureaus are a valid expression of an individual's Credit Character.

* *In statistical terms, a credit risk score predicts the probability that a consumer will become 90 days overdue (or greater) on any given account over the next 24 months.*

How is the Credit Score Calculated?

The credit score is the outcome of a complex process based on statistical modules. These modules, developed and refined over decades, process the thousands of data points which are present in the credit file of an individual.

Credit-scoring systems were originally designed for lenders, not consumers. This means that credit scores continue to be difficult to understand. Actual formulae and details of how credit scores work are closely guarded trade secrets.

There are constant changes in the data pertaining to consumers. In order to be accurate, the scorecard (statistical model that calculates the credit score) takes all these changes into account. Built to be dynamic, the score is able to assess risk based on the changes that occur inevitably over time, in every person's credit profile.

There are several factors which impact a person's credit profile.

1. Payment history (covering all current and past records and delinquency, if any)
2. Amount owed
3. Length of credit history
4. New credit
5. Types of credit

Credit Scores in India

- **Every credit bureau in India uses its own scoring logic to generate credit scores. Equifax, CIBIL, Experian and Highmark all have their own credit scorecards**

- Credit scores can vary for the same individual from one credit bureau to another. This has been a major source of confusion for underwriters and applicants alike
- In 2015, based on a committee set up by the Reserve Bank of India, all credit scores in India were required to be in the same range (300–900)
- Individual credit bureau scores can vary from one bureau to another (depending upon the scoring logic). However, these have to range between 300 and 900
- CIBIL provides a score with a range of 1–5 to all those who are new to credit and have credit history spanning less than 6 months
- An individual without any credit history is given a score of "NA/NH" by CIBIL. This denotes any one or a combination of the following situations:
    - One does not have any credit history or does not have adequate credit history to be scored
    - All the credit facilities of the individual are closed and he has not availed any new loan or credit facility
    - The individual has only add-on cards
- Unlike CIBIL, Equifax assigns scores even to those who individuals do not have any credit history. This is based on various factors such as peer group performance

Payment History

"Payment history" is a log of all current and past repayments of a borrower. The regularity of the borrower on repayments before the due dates is what forms the basis of this parameter. Has the borrower paid all his dues in time? Has he delayed payments? How recent are these delays? The answers to all of these questions impact an individual's payment history. Other factors influencing this parameter are the types of credit products where the borrower has defaulted and the duration of such defaults.

Amount Owed

This parameter measures how much of his available credit limit an individual has utilized. It also takes into account the total amount which is owed by an individual apart from how much an individual currently owes in relation to the amount originally borrowed.

As recently as the mid-1990s, many South African credit scores considered the color of the borrower's skin. Lower scores would be calculated for colored consumers!

Length of Credit History

This factor is based on the length of time each account has remained open and the accounts' most recent action. As a result, it is difficult for a person who is new to credit to have a great credit score. A longer credit history provides more information and offers more insights into an individual's long-term credit behavior.

New Credit

This factor takes into account the time elapsed since the last credit facility was sanctioned by any lending institution. It also factors in the amount approved and the type of credit facility/ loan.

Types of Credit

This factor takes into account the variety of credit facilities an individual has currently or has availed in the past. A good credit mix is indicative of the fact that the borrower can handle all types of credit. Historical data indicates that borrowers with a good blend of all types of credit generally represent a lower level of risk for lenders.

What is a Good Credit Score?

Credit Scores in India ranges from 300 to 900 irrespective of the credit bureau from which these are generated. A score of 750 and above is considered to be good score. As per the CIBIL website, about 79% of loans or credit cards being disbursed are to borrowers having a score above 750.

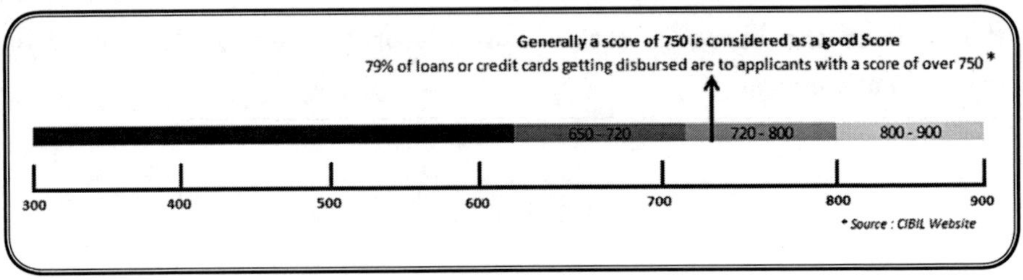

Credit Score range in India

FICO

The FICO score is the scoring module developed and named after the company called FICO (Erstwhile Fair, Isaac & Company). Introduced in 1989, the model is used by three major credit bureaus in the USA (Equifax, Experian and TransUnion) apart from several other bureaus.

The FICO score assesses the risk profile of an individual by using various details available on record. FICO records both negative and positive data reported by banks or lenders to the bureau. The data is divided into five categories to calculate the credit score. The table below denotes these factors along with their impact on the FICO score. Please note that these percentages are valid in the US context.

Factors influencing the FICO Score

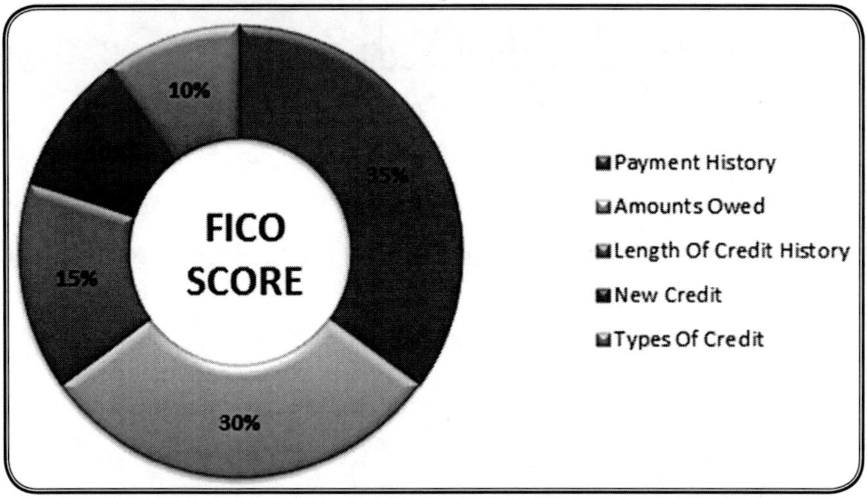

FICO is the most widely used scorecard in USA (it claims to be used in 90% of underwriting decisions). FICO is present in India and provides analytical support to various businesses.

If Your Credit Score Is.....	This Is How You Fare.....
800 or above	Excellent score. You will be a preferred customer for the lenders
750 to 800	Good score. Lenders will look at your application favorably
700 to 750	Fair score. Secured lending might be possible but unsecured loans are likely to be priced higher for the risk involved
600 to 700	Poor. In exceptional cases, a secured loan might get sanctioned
Less Than 600	Very poor. No loan or credit facility is likely to be provided by any prime lender

How does the Credit Score impact Loan/Credit Applications?

The illustration given below demonstrates how the credit score impacts the decision process of any credit application. Every application has to meet the minimum credit score benchmark.

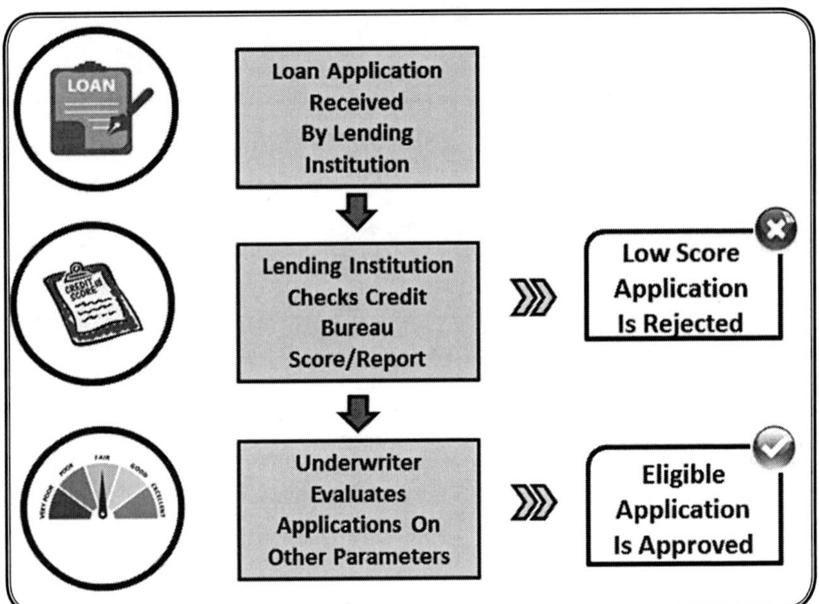

Impact of Credit Score on a Loan Application

Only those applications which meet the minimum credit criteria get assessed by an underwriter. Different lending institutions could have different benchmarks for the same product and the same institutions could have different minimum criteria for different products. Some lending institutions use the credit score in conjunction with the credit report. Credit applications which do not meet the minimum criteria could get rejected without further decision-making steps (especially in the case of an unsecured product).

How can you Obtain your Credit Score?

Obtaining a credit score is a fairly simple process. It takes only a few minutes for an individual to generate his credit report and score.

Individuals may access their credit reports in any of the following ways:

1. Obtain a free credit bureau score and report (from Equifax) by visiting www.freescoreindia.com . Submit basic information about yourself including your PAN and Aadhar number. After you submit these, your credit report will be generated. A notification is sent to you once the report is ready.
2. Obtain a copy of the report from the lending institution where you have (*if you have*) applied for a loan. An applicant can ask for a copy of the credit report (based on which the bank has decided on the loan request)*. However, this report may not contain complete information on all the credit facilities.
3. Obtain the credit report by visiting any of the credit bureau websites. While some of the bureaus have an online process, individuals may have to submit KYC (identity and address proof) documents along with the requisite payment to obtain their credit reports. The cost of the report varies from one bureau to another: CIBIL (Rs. 500), Equifax (Rs. 400), Experian (Rs. 399) and Highmark (Rs. 299).

---

* As per the Credit Information Company Act, the bank may charge for this service.

Common Credit Report and Score Misconceptions

There are several misconceptions surrounding a credit score. Some of these are a result of an acute lack of awareness while others are carefully cultivated myths based on a limited understanding of the subject.

1. My credit score will drop if I check it

   Checking your own score has no impact on it. You can check your score every day if you so desire (Refer to the box on Hard v/s Soft Inquiries).

2. My credit score gets impacted by my place of living

   In general, demographic factors including place of living, do not play any role in credit scoring models.

"Hard" v/s "Soft" Inquiries

- "Hard" inquiries are requests for credit reports that can affect your credit score. A hard inquiry shows up on the credit report and indicates that you are actively trying to get credit in the form of a housing loan, personal loan, car loan, credit card or in some other form.
- "Soft" inquiries, on the other hand, do not affect your score. They do not reflect on the credit report. Such inquiries are not the result of banks checking the bureau to obtain information on an applicant's credit profile. For example, when you check your own credit score, it is a soft inquiry. Similarly, a lending institution may review the accounts of existing borrowers from time to time. This account review does not affect your credit score.

3. Being a co-borrower has no impact on my credit score

   The credit/loan details reflect in all co-borrowers' bureau reports. Being a co borrower has an impact similar to any other credit relationship.

4. As the guarantor of a loan, I do not need to worry about the repayment of the loan and its impact on my credit score

   You do not need to worry about being a guarantor till the time the loan is being repaid promptly. However, in the event of default, it becomes your liability to repay the loan. Failure to do so will impact your credit score.

Factors that do NOT generally Impact your Credit Score

- Income level
- Education level
- Religion, race, nationality
- Gender or marital status
- Age
- Employment or occupation history
- Inquiry made by you to obtain your own credit report
- Location of residence or length of stay at one place
- Wealth levels

5. Paying in cash for my purchases (rather than using my credit card) will help me build my credit score

   A cash transaction does not have any impact on your credit score. On the contrary, if you use a credit card to buy a product or service it may have a positive impact on your credit score (provided you pay back in time on this card and other accounts as well)

6. Utility bills payments have a bearing on my credit score

   Currently, in India, utility bills do not have any bearing on the credit score. Even so, it is advisable to pay all your bills in time.

7. My score will be excellent if I do not have any credit cards or loans

   Not having any credit accounts means that you do not have any credit history. Your credit history is vital to bureaus because this data is used by them to generate your credit scores. Contrary to popular perception, you are likely to have no score if you do not have any credit facilities (no history).

8. The negative accounts on my credit report purge after 7 years and have no impact on my credit score

   In some countries, delinquent accounts do get purged after a stipulated time frame (normally 7 years). The regulations in India are silent on this aspect. A loan or credit facility with missed payments is likely to continue to reflect on the bureau report and impact your credit score (irrespective of how long ago they have been closed).

New Frontiers in Credit Scoring

Traditional Credit Scoring models use bureau data to generate a credit score. Bureau data consists of data contributed by lending institutions (and in some countries, data on utility payments as well). Statistically, traditional scoring models use only a fraction of the information that pertains to any individual. This has led to the development of credit scoring models using large data (big data) sources such as social media networks and mobile usage statistics. While the usage of such scoring models has yet to attain any significant momentum, there is reason to believe that using traditional score cards in conjunction with "big data" could benefit underwriters substantially.

Social Credit Score

A large number of individuals have an online life and increasingly more and more people are joining online social media networks. The social credit score assesses an individual based on the data available on various online platforms and applications like Facebook, LinkedIn and other social media. The assessment of the credit worthiness of an individual is based on a variety of factors such as the depth of the individual's network and the quality and quantity of social interactions.

Score on Mobile Usage

There are over 1 billion mobile users globally who do not feature on the credit bureaus. While they may have jobs, there is no credit history for them. The usage patterns of their mobile phones could prove to be a vast source of information about the users' ability to repay debts and use credit responsibly.

Uses of Credit Scores

Credit Scores have an impact on several facets of our lives. Some of these aspects are mentioned below. It is to be noted here that some of the "non-lending" implications mentioned might have a limited applicability in the current Indian context. (Refer Box on page 48)

1. Approval for loan or credit applications :

   Reviewing credit character is one of the first steps in the decision-making process of an underwriter.

2. Interest rate charged on a credit facility :

   An individual with a riskier credit profile is likely to be charged a higher rate of interest than a person with a lower risk profile.

3. Loan amount against value of collateral :

   A borrower with a good credit profile may be able to unlock the value of his collateral to a greater extent than a borrower with a poor credit profile.

Impact of Credit Score on Loan Amount

Applicant	Credit Score	Property Value (Rs)	Loan Disbursed (Rs)	Interest Charged
Mr. A	803	100,00,000	60,00,000	12%
Mr. B	687	100,00,000	32,00,000	15%

In the above example, both Mr. A and Mr. B are looking for home loans. Mr. A is able to get a loan for 60% of the property value but Mr. B has been provided only 32% of the property value as loan. There is also a difference in the rate of interest charged (3%) between Mr. A and Mr. B.

This example, which highlights the difference in loan amounts and interest rates (based on credit scores), is the most direct use of credit scores, especially in the Indian context. However, the world over, credit scores affect several other areas of our lives.

4. Employment opportunities

   Employers often check on the credit score prior to hiring a candidate. This is usually a part of the background check performed by employers to ascertain the candidate's credit character. Such checks do require the candidate's consent.

The Delhi High Court, on 14.01.2015, in the case titled Kusum Sharma v Mahinder Kumar Sharma, reported as AIR 2015 DELHI 53, has passed a judgement on a matter relating to the formulation of format of affidavit of assets, income and expenditure to help the courts in determining the true income, expenditure of parties and to decide on the amount of maintenance. In this matter, an amicus curiae (friend of the court) submitted that the report of CIBIL provided a complete insight into the person's liabilities including loans and repayments and it gave a clear indication of the financial position of a person. She recommended that a report of CIBIL be filed along with the relevant affidavit. Accepting the suggestion, the High Court, under Part X of the Affidavit, under the head, 'Documents relating to income, assets and liabilities', has required the CIBIL report to be attached along with other documents.

---

5. Telecom connections

   Telecommunication companies often perform checks on an individual's credit profile prior to approving a new connection. The credit score in this case may impact the telecom plan made available to the applicant and the cost of the plan. A person with a low score might have to pay higher call charges compared to a person with a high credit score. It is also possible that a service provider may even decline the connection request completely, based on the credit profile.

There is an online dating service called CreditScoreDating.com for those who would like to check on the financial situation of a potential partner. The site's motto is "Credit Scores Are Sexy."

---

6. Insurance coverage/premium

   Insurance companies commonly use consumer credit information in conjunction with the data normally used for underwriting an insurance cover. The credit information influences the premium charged on the policy.

7. Property rental decisions

   A landlord would, without doubt, want to rent out his property to a person with a sound financial background. No landlord would want to rent out his property to someone who might default on the rental payments, or worse still, end up illegally occupying his property. Checking the credit report of a prospective tenant helps the landlord to decide if he would turn out to be a responsible tenant or not.

Use of Credit Bureaus for non-lending decisions in India

Telecom services providers:

Some telecom service providers use bureau data to evaluate the credit limit offered to consumers on post-paid connections. Often, such decisions are based on proprietary scorecards (developed by the telecom service providers) which make use of bureau information.

Insurance Companies:

Affluence Indicators: Insurance companies in India have started to use "affluence Indicator scorecards" based on bureau data to underwrite new insurance policies. This scorecard helps the insurance companies to decide on the sum assured based on "surrogates" for income without actually having to ask customers for income documents.

Retention Management:

"Lapsation" of policies is a major challenge confronting insurance companies in India. Setting priorities on a large pool of lapsed policies, so as to reinstate them, can be a daunting task. Insurance companies use bureau information to make informed choices in this regard which help them to prioritize, improve targeting efficiency and save costs.

Employment:

Background checks: Several companies in India are using credit reports as part of the background check of a prospective employee. Currently, this trend is more prevalent in the financial services sector. However, it is likely to become more common place with increased awareness of the costs associated with employee fraud and wrong hiring decisions.

8. Utility services

   Utility service providers normally provide their consumers with a credit period within which they can pay their bills. A credit bureau report helps in ascertaining how responsible an individual is towards his obligations. Individuals with a low credit score may be charged a higher rental or usage fee. In some cases, they may be asked to put up a deposit with the service provider which could be offset (in case of default on payments) against unpaid dues.

A Good Credit Score: The Key to a Hidden Fortune

In today's world, economies are increasingly driven by consumption demand. We spend money on various products and services which fulfil our needs and aspirations. When we wish to buy a product where the costs are high; like a car, we have only two options. We can either take a loan or we can save money to buy it outright. The following are the questions that need to be answered in this context:

- How long will one have to save money in order to accumulate enough money to buy a car?
- Even if one does achieve the targeted savings goal, will he be able to buy the car? Perhaps not, since the price of the car would have increased on account of inflation (increase in the cost of the car on account of a hike in the price of raw materials/labor and other inputs) that the individual had not factored in.
- Is it worth saving and investing money in a depreciating asset where the value of the car diminishes the moment it gets rolled out of a dealer's showroom?

While it is still possible that an individual may be able to buy a car from money saved, but what about buying a property (either for living or for investment), or if the funding is required to expand one's business ?

There is only so much that can be achieved from the limited capital available with any individual. It is, therefore, important to be credit healthy in order to have access to loans and other credit facilities.

In this context, a good credit score could be the key to a hidden fortune. Our consumption, investment and savings goals depend on our ability to avail different types of credit facilities.

A good score helps to access the following critically important aspects of our financial lives such as:

a) Availability of funding when we need it the most

b) Lower rates of interest on credit facilities

India has a large middle class population and typically most of the families would want to buy a house, car and invest in education. It may be presumed that such households would avail at least one home loan, four or five car loans and two personal loans to meet their requirements over a life time.

The interest charged to a borrower on each of these loans would be a function of the risk associated with the borrower. Since the score is reflective of the risk involved in the lending process, it has an obvious impact on the interest rates associated with the credit facility. The higher the credit score, the lower the associated risk and the lower the rate of interest on the loan.

Being credit healthy results in huge savings in the interest paid on loans

Loan Type	No Of Loans In Life	Savings
Home Loan	1	12,09,001
Car Loan	5	1,19,688
Personal/Education Loan	2	1,62,238
Total Savings		14,90,927

Home Loan	Interest @ 10%	Interest @ 11%
Loan Amount	75,00,000	75,00,000
Loan years	20	20
Total Amount Paid	1,73,70,390	1,85,79,391

Car Loan	Interest @ 10%	Interest @ 12%
Loan Amount	5,00,000	5,00,000
Loan years	5	5
Total Amount Paid	6,37,411	6,67,333

Personal Loan	Interest @ 15%	Interest @ 20%
Loan Amount	5,00,000	5,00,000
Loan years	5	5
Total Amount Paid	7,13,698	7,94,817

All figures are in Rs.

Higher Score = Higher Savings

The table above illustrates the savings potential of a higher credit score over a lifetime (assuming the credit requirements to be one Housing Loan, five Car Loans and two Personal Loans). The savings opportunity available to a credit healthy individual could be as high as 14-15 lacs!

While this fact may not be immediately apparent to most people, this savings opportunity could be one of the biggest motivations of staying credit healthy over a lifetime.

Moreover, good credit health fills us with a sense of pride and self-respect which is critical to financial freedom.

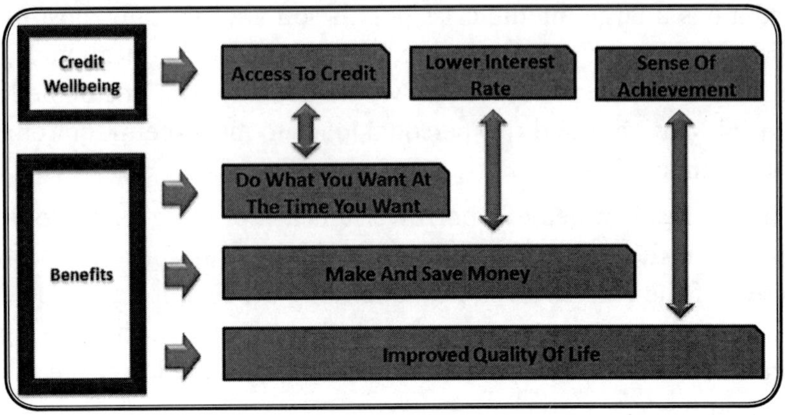

Benefits of being Credit Healthy

Being credit healthy is a way of life. Just as being physically healthy demands a daily regimen based on awareness of its importance; good credit is about recognizing its potential and taking concrete steps in this direction.

Key Points

- A credit report is a comprehensive chronicle of an individual's credit history.
- Credit scores are a numerical measure of a person's Credit Character
- A free credit report may be obtained by visiting www.freescoreindia.com
- There are 5 main factors affecting the credit score namely: payment history, account balances, vintage of the credit account/s, credit mix and inquiries
- Credit scores impact us in several spheres of life including the access to credit to fund our growing needs
- A good credit score can save us lacs of rupees in interest costs every year
- Being credit healthy is a way of life : concrete steps in this direction can lead us to financial freedom

PART III

Tips for Being Credit Healthy

TIP-I

Review your Credit Regularly

Samir Malik

Samir works as a medical representative in a pharmaceutical company. Both his parents are working in government jobs. He stays with them in a government provided accommodation. Samir is hard working and normally earns handsome incentives over and above his fixed salary. He is single and does not need to contribute towards household expenses. Samir has been meticulous in spending only the fixed salary component of his income and saving all his incentives. He has been able to save about 3 lakh rupees.

Samir has two credit cards and uses them very sparingly. One of the cards that he received when he was a student has not been used even once. Now that he is getting married, he intends to avail of a personal loan for his wedding expenses. To his dismay, his personal loan application gets rejected for a low credit score.

Samir is in a fix. Why should his credit score be low when he has never ever defaulted on his credit facilities?

Joseph D'Souza

Joseph is a well-to- do business consultant who specializes in process reengineering to save costs for his clients and make them more customer centric. He is 34 years old and is paid very well by his company. Joseph has two credit cards apart from a home loan. He drives a car, the loan on which has been paid off completely two years ago. Now, Joseph wishes to buy a new car. After identifying a luxury car, he applies for a loan that gets declined. He is shocked to discover that an unpaid personal loan is reflecting in his credit bureau report. The loan had apparently been disbursed about 8 months ago and has not been paid for the last 6 months.

The bank communicates its inability to provide Joseph a loan till he clears the default on the personal loan account and improves his credit score!

Such instances are commonplace. Few people realize the importance of credit scores until they are declined by a lending institution for a credit facility or start getting collection calls. So, how does one avoid such unpleasant surprises?

Such situations can only be avoided through regular reviews of your credit report. And if you have not reviewed your credit report yet, this is the right time to make a start!

Reviewing your report helps in four important ways:

1. Making a beginning to a credit healthy life
2. Maintaining good credit health
3. Assisting in achieving financial goals
4. Identifying errors on the credit report

Make a Beginning

A beginning is the first required step towards achieving a desirable end to any objective. Just like knowing about your current physical status is required to make a beginning on the journey of being physically healthy, knowing about your current credit health status is the first step towards embarking on a financially healthy life.

The first step in this direction is to obtain a credit bureau report and become aware of its contents (we have mentioned ways to obtain your credit report and score in an earlier chapter). Doing so can help avoid consequences that can be devastating, as is seen in the case studies of Samir and Joseph.

Maintaining Good Credit Health

Once you have made a start, it is imperative to review the credit report regularly. But how would a regular review help? Can't one review his credit status just before applying for a credit facility?

Obtaining your first report is like going to the gym and assessing your current physical condition on various parameters. Consistent exercise thereafter is indispensable for you to gain the benefits of physical wellness. Similarly, maintaining consistency in reviewing your report is essential to maintaining good credit health.

Regularity on this front will help to keep you abreast with the changes in your credit score. This, then, can facilitate a better understanding on how different parameters may impact your credit score.

Credit scores are dynamic in nature. Since the score is an outcome of various parameters that keep changing, it is important to review the reports at periodic intervals. If one does so regularly, he will be able to identify areas of improvement. This helps to manage and maintain a good credit score.

Please note that credit reports state only the facts available with the bureau (perceived to be factual until an error is identified) and only a review can help to get insights into the factors that impact your credibility; or shall we say your financial goals!

How often should I check my credit report?

A monthly review of your credit report is recommended by the authors. You can set up a particular date every month to review your report.

Assist in Saving Money

All of us have financial goals which revolve around saving money for the future. A Regular review of your credit report can unravel savings opportunities by benchmarking existing credit facilities against products currently available in the market. This could help to refinance existing credit facilities (from the existing lending institution) to a lower cost provider. While such reviews and switches may be challenging to execute for the uninitiated, but with expert help they could turn into habits which will help you to achieve your financial goals.

Identifying Errors on the Credit Report

As seen in Joseph's case study, the consequences of an error on a credit report can be distressing and can adversely impact our financial plans. Regular reviews help us to identify errors at an early stage and take corrective action. Any delay in identifying and rectifying errors can negatively impact our credit score.

A large number of credit reports have errors. Hence, a regular check would not only ensure that your information is getting updated correctly but also help you to detect fraudulent activities or identity theft issues at an early stage.

An error can lead an underwriter to reject a loan application on the basis of a faulty credit report. It may result, at times, in higher interest rates getting charged. It is, therefore, important to have such errors corrected as soon as possible. Timely correction of errors helps to ensure access to credit at the time when it is needed the most.

Dispute Resolution

This is what you should do when you identify errors on your credit report:

1. Call up the customer care of the concerned lending institution and lodge a complaint. Do ask for a service request/complaint number.
2. Send out a mail referencing the service request/complaint number (in the subject line) detailing the issue being addressed to the grievance redressal officer (details of each lending institution's grievance redressal officer are available on their website).
3. The mail sent to the grievance redressal officer should also be copied to the concerned credit bureau.
4. As per the Credit Information Act, you should get a response within 30 days of your communication to the grievance redressal officer.
5. Once the response on the correct update is received, the same should be sent across to the credit bureau for rectification.
6. In the event of not receiving a response or in the event of not receiving a satisfactory resolution from the lending institution, the issue may be escalated to the Banking Ombudsman (BO). The Banking

Ombudsman is a senior official appointed by the Reserve Bank of India. The role of the Ombudsman is to act on customer complaints pertaining to deficiency in banking services.

7. In the event of not being satisfied with the resolution provided by the Banking Ombudsman, the borrower can make an appeal to the Deputy Governor of the RBI. He can reject the appeal, modify the order of the BO or send it back to the BO for review.
8. A borrower has the right to move the matter to a consumer court in case he is not satisfied even after the intervention of the RBI.

Credit Scoring Errors

Imagine a situation where you sign up for a blood test and the report is wrong. The implications of such an error could be very damaging and even fatal, at times. Similarly, an error on a credit report has the potential to impact your financial wellbeing quite adversely. Underwriting decisions are based on the information available on a credit report. The approval of loans, the interest rate to be charged, and the loan amount sanctioned are all based on the underwriter's assessment of an individual's credit worthiness which, in turn, is based on the assumption of an accurate and updated credit report.

How do credit report errors occur?

A credit report error may be defined as the inclusion of incorrect information or exclusion of correct information on a credit report.

A credit report may have errors due to the following reasons:

1. Erroneous reporting by lending institutions :

   In India, we have over 1000 lending institutions comprising large private sector banks, public sector banks, cooperative banks, Gramin banks, NBFCs and other private lending institutions. All these institutions are required to report data in a prescribed format. Notwithstanding this, the quality of data that is submitted to bureaus is often non- standardized and is not updated with recent changes. The frequency of reporting (while mandated to be at least once in 30 days) also leads to situations where there is a lag between reporting and the actual changes in an individual's account status.

2. Algorithmic constraints :

   Credit bureaus function by collecting account level information about the borrowers from lending institutions. A credit report is generated based on this information using an algorithm. This algorithm involves using a person's name and other unique identifiers such as PAN number and Aadhar number to match and identify all the accounts that are available with the credit bureau. But problems arise when the algorithm mistakenly matches one person's overdue account to another person with a similar name. This is further compounded by the lack of unique identifiers in India (such as Social Security Numbers- SSN in the USA)

3. Identity Fraud :

   Identity Fraud happens when someone illegally uses another individual's identity and credentials to obtain a loan. In such cases, the report itself may be depicting information as reported by the lending institution. The onus is on the person with the wrong credit report to prove that he is the victim of identity fraud. In the meantime, the account continues to get reported on the credit bureau.

This type of "error" is very serious since the victim of identity fraud can be clueless about this unless he checks on his credit report regularly.

Globally, the error rates on credit reports are high. According to a study in the USA, one fourth of all consumers identified an error on their credit bureau reports[*].

In India the error rates are even higher. According to a consumer credit survey conducted in India, one out of three reports has errors[**].

Of the 28 crore individuals' data stored on any of India's credit bureaus, it is unnerving to even imagine that there could be errors on about 9 crore consumers' data[***].

---

* Federal Trade Commission survey results published in Feb 2013

** Consumer Survey results published by Credit Sudhaar in Dec 2013 in eight major cities of India

*** Based on an extrapolation of the sampling survey results. Such extrapolation may require further validation

Classification of Errors

Errors on a credit report can be classified into two categories: Minor errors and Major errors.

A minor error comprises errors in address, name (including spelling), mobile number or email id. These errors do not impact the credit score. However, a major error, pertaining to one's identification numbers, account information, credit history, loan amounts and credit inquiries can impact the credit score in a significant manner.

The same survey which indicated that one out of three reports has errors also went on to state that over 70% of these errors are of a major nature.

With such high occurrences of errors in general (and major errors in particular), it becomes imperative for everyone to watch out for errors in their credit report and get these corrected. One more very good reason to review your credit regularly!

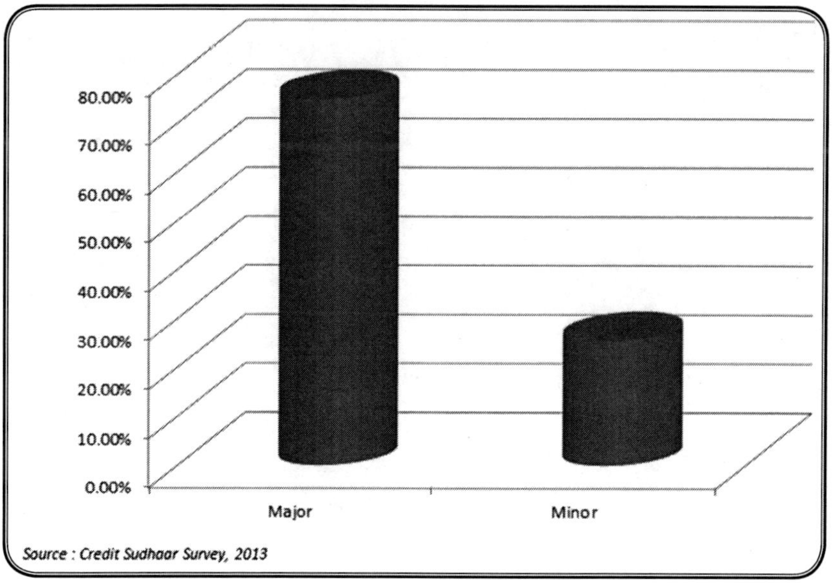

Credit Bureau Errors in India

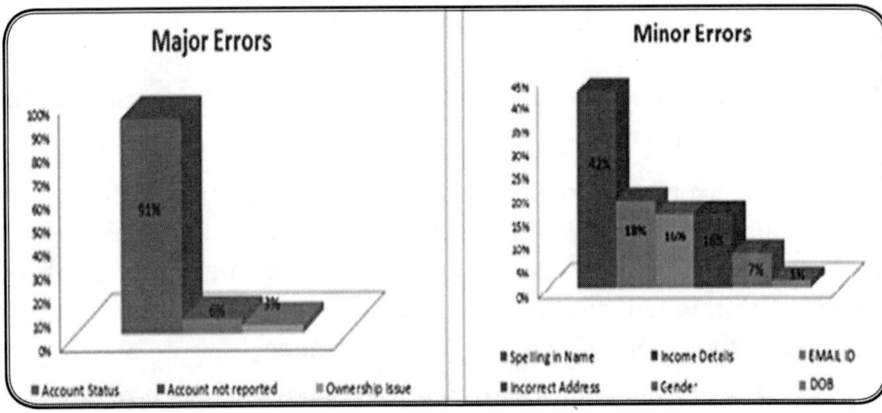

Source : Credit Sudhaar Survey, 2013

Major & Minor Error Bifurcation

Types of Credit Bureau Errors

Key Points

- Reviewing credit reports regularly is the first step towards credit awareness
- It is estimated that one third of credit bureau reports in India have errors
- Regular reviews of your credit report help in several ways:
  - Making a beginning to a credit healthy life
  - Maintaining good credit health
  - Assisting in achieving financial goals
  - Identifying errors on the credit report.
- Errors on credit reports can have a devastating impact on an individual's credit health
- Set up a credit check up day every month and a "to do" list to act on items that need attention

TIP-II

Have a Good Credit Mix

Iqbal Singh

Iqbal is a cardiologist by profession and has a flourishing practice. He lives in a high end inherited apartment and drives a BMW that he had bought with his own money (not a loan). He has only one credit card, the outstanding on which he always pays in full before the monthly due date. Recently, Iqbal applied for a personal loan and his application was rejected. Surprised, he inquired with the bank and was informed that he had a low credit score. Iqbal pulled out his credit report and was shocked to see his score at a low of 517.

Notwithstanding Iqbal's financial stature, he was rejected for a loan on account of a low credit score. Why was his score low?

Often, people think that having no loans or credit cards (or not using credit cards at all); will help them to have a good credit score. This is far from the truth. Inadequate number of credit accounts or limited usage of credit facilities implies that the bureau has limited data to score you. This has the impact of actually lowering your credit score!

Types of Credit

There are primarily two types of credit – **Revolving Credit** and **Term Credit** (also called non-revolving/fixed term credit).

Term Credit refers to the credit products that have a fixed repayment period. This means that the loan duration is decided prior to disbursal and the borrower is expected to repay the complete loan amount within the stipulated period. The value of the monthly repayment in these products is usually fixed.

Revolving Credit refers to credit products where the repayment duration is not fixed and the borrower has the flexibility to continue with the account as long as he wishes (with some limitations) and also decide on the repayment amount.

Credit may also be classified in a different manner: **Secured Credit and Unsecured Credit.**

Secured Credit refers to credit products where an asset is given as security against the loan. In the event of a default, the lender has the right to sell the asset and recover the money.

Unsecured Credit refers to credit products where no collateral is provided as security against a loan.

The table below illustrates different types of credit with examples.

	Term	**Revolving**
Secured	• Home Loan • Loan Against Property • Large Ticket Business Loan • Gold Loan • Car Loan • Education Loan • Loan Against Shares • Consumer Durable Loan	• Secured Over Draft • Secured Credit Card
Unsecured	• Personal Loan • Small Ticket Business Loan • Education Loan	• Over draft • Credit Card

Each of these credit types is associated with a different risk perception for a lending institution. Loans secured by collateral carry the least risk. Unsecured loans such as credit cards and personal loans are associated with higher risk as the lending institution has no recourse to collateral in the event of default.

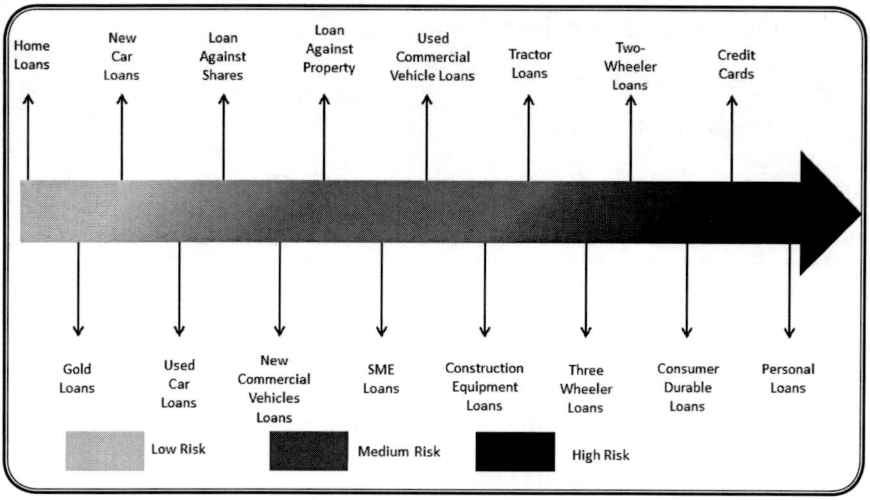

Risk continuum for different types of Credit

Good Credit Mix

Having a good mix of all types of credit is as important to your credit score as a balanced and nutritious diet is to achieving good physical health.

A good mix of credit involves having a mix of different types of credit spanning the risk continuum, including unsecured and secured products apart from revolving and term credit.

Ideal Credit Mix

The authors have often been asked questions on what constitutes an ideal credit mix. The answer to this question depends on a number of factors including the financial background and life stage of an individual. Such factors vary from person to person. It is only by studying the concerned person's particular circumstances that one can come to any meaningful conclusion about his ideal credit mix. Nevertheless, the following is a generic recommendation of an ideal account mix that one is advised to have at any point of time.

1. **One secured term loan**
2. **One unsecured term loan**
3. **Three credit cards**

All of the above refer to active credit accounts. Closed credit lines should not be included in this mix.

Coming back to Iqbal's example, his loan application was rejected despite having a flourishing business and never having defaulted on his credit cards.

- Iqbal did not have any credit accounts apart from a credit card
- Iqbal rarely used his credit card
- Iqbal's credit bureau report did not display a mix of different types of credit
- All of the above factors led to a low credit score for Iqbal

What should Iqbal do?

The recommendations for Iqbal are as follows:

- Firstly, Iqbal should apply for at least two more credit cards and use them. However, he should be careful not to use these cards for more than 40% of the credit limit
- Iqbal should avail a vehicle loan to buy his next car (rather than make a cash down payment)

Over time, these steps should help Iqbal to have a better credit mix and improve his credit score.

Make an early start with Credit

Similar to starting to save as soon as one gets his first pay cheque, getting started with credit early in life has its own set of advantages. An early starter would be able to build a good credit history over time and thus shall be viewed favorably when in need of larger and more complex loans.

- A person can start with credit cards and use them wisely.
- As time progresses, one should look at buying a vehicle by availing a loan.

Credit For those Who are Not able To Get it

Everyone needs to have access to credit (and a good credit mix); even those who have had a history of delinquency (which compromises their credit character). Paradoxically, credit is usually available only to those who have good credit character. However, there are a few options available to those people who need credit but find it difficult to convince lending institutions to take a credit risk on them.

Debt Consolidation

Debt consolidation is a loan product where the current outstanding amounts (owed to various lending institutions) get combined into a single account. Such debt consolidation loans are usually secured by some form of collateral.

Secured Credit Cards

Secured cards are credit cards issued against fixed deposits. The applicant has to book a fixed deposit against which a limit (typically up to 90%) is provided on a secured card. This card functions like any other credit card. Since it is secured by a fixed deposit, these are relatively easy to acquire, even for those people who have poor credit.

Gold Loans

In the case of a gold loan, the borrower has to put up gold (which he needs to have at his disposal) as security, against which a loan is sanctioned. Irrespective of their credit status, most Indian households are likely to have some gold. This makes a gold loan an accessible credit facility for those who want to unlock the value of this asset.

Key Points

- There are several types of credit: term credit and revolving credit; unsecured credit and secured credit
- A good credit mix can be defined as a situation where the borrower is able to display good repayment on all types of credit facilities (term/revolving and secured/unsecured types of credit)
- Ideal Credit Mix : It is recommended that one should have at least three revolving credit accounts, apart from one secured and unsecured credit account, to have a good mix of credit
- Get started with credit early in your adult life and add different types of credit as time progresses

TIP-III

Resolve Mistakes Made in the Past

"Everyone makes mistakes. That's why there is an eraser at the end of every pencil"

Somesh Singh

Somesh Singh hails from a middle class family. Somesh has spent all his childhood in a rented accommodation. His father, who has now retired from his government job, worked hard to ensure that his children received a good education.

Somesh now works as a supervisor with an international BPO. He is married and his wife works with a private institution. They have a child who was born about a year ago.

Three years ago, Somesh was promoted as a team leader and to avoid long travelling hours, he shifted to another rented accommodation closer to his current workplace.

Somesh had a childhood desire to stay in his own house. About 3 years ago, Somesh took a housing loan on an under construction property. His wife became a co-borrower to the loan. The developer had promised to deliver the house in about a year's time. However, the developer had not lived up to his promise and had been regularly postponing delivery deadlines.

Meanwhile, Somesh's sister's marriage got fixed and the wedding expenses were met from the retirement benefits of his father. Somesh also took a small personal loan to help his father out. Soon after his sister's marriage, Somesh's child was born and his expenses shot up. The regular vaccination, medical and other expenses stretched his credit cards' usage to the maximum limit.

Somesh now has to pay rent apart from the home loan EMI. He has to service a personal loan EMI and the outstanding on his credit card. Given the fact that a large portion of his father's fixed deposit (from his retirement benefits) was withdrawn for his sister's marriage, the steady interest income that supported his parents' expenses has also gone down. Now, Somesh also needs to contribute towards his parents' living expenses.

Somesh is unable to meet his expenses and pay all his dues (loan EMIs and credit card bills.

Rajab Mohle

Rajab Mohle joined an IT firm through a campus placement with a monthly salary of Rs. 60,000 per month. Excited about the job and his career prospects, he shifted to Bangalore where the firm was headquartered. He rented a two bedroom apartment, thinking that he should have a room for his parents as and when they visit him. He was issued one credit card from the bank where he had his salary account and also applied for cards from two other banks. An avid biker at heart, Somesh bought a high end bike by availing a loan.

Buoyed by his job, Rajab started living life "king size". He spent regularly on expensive brands, outings and foreign holidays. Gradually the outstanding on his credit cards started to mount and Rajab was unable to pay the total outstanding every month. This continued for a few months till he had used the maximum assigned limits on his credit cards. Over time, the outstanding amounts breached the maximum limits. Along with the high rental outflow and the EMI on his bike, he started to pay only the minimum amount due on his card. Because of the high interest rates and other charges that got levied, the outstanding on Rajab's card never really reduced.

Rajab was in a fix. High living costs and mounting debts were taking a toll on his finances. He started getting calls from banks to bring his card outstanding down. One of the banks revised his credit limit downwards. Unable to manage his funds, he shared his concern with one of his friends who advised him to stop paying his credit card dues and settle the outstanding in the next 3 to 4 months. Rajab was given to understand (by his friend) that this would enable him to negotiate with his bank on the interest charges that had been levied.

Rajab went ahead and followed the advice and closed all his credit cards and even settled the outstanding amounts with the bank.

Reasons for Default

People default on their credit facilities primarily on account of the following reasons:

- Ineffective management of funds (income) and inability to manage expenses:
  As we saw in Somesh's case, he was unable to administer and manage his funds and hence got into a default situation. Budgeting and managing expenses within one's income is very important in this context. While in general, people do attempt to manage their funds, but the lack of a systematic approach in this matter leads to situations which cause default.
- Unforeseen Circumstances:
  At times, certain exigencies such as medical expenses, job loss, business downturn or similar circumstances lead to a gap between sources and uses of funds, causing an individual to default.
- Limited awareness and lack of understanding of how credit products function:
  The lack of understanding of the features, functionalities of credit product is another reason for people to default. In India, the lack of credit literacy and the absence of effective bureaus has been a significant reason for people to default (rather than the defaults triggered by the onset of unforeseen circumstances)*.

Indeed, the case studies of Somesh and Rajab are clear examples of self-inflicted credit traps rather than any unexpected financial shocks which derailed them from the path of credit health.

Irrespective of the reason for default, navigating out of a default situation requires a systematic plan to correct mistakes made in the past.

Navigating out of Default: A Systematic Plan

A systematic plan to make good on the mistakes of the past involves the following steps:

---

* Refer to Chapter 1: The Great Indian Retail Meltdown

1. Recognize your mistakes – don't live in denial
2. Take corrective action with your finances : tighten your belt
3. Know your rights
4. Ask your creditors for a helping hand

Recognize Your Mistakes

As credit professionals, the authors have come across innumerable instances where people do not recognize non-payment or short payment to lenders as a mistake. The accountability regarding obligations towards lending institutions is often not viewed with adequate seriousness. Various credit misconceptions and the lack of awareness fuel this attitude. It is not uncommon to hear statements such as the ones below:

- "What's the big deal if I did not pay my dues before changing my city or residence? It is the bank's job to contact me for their dues."
- "Payment delays of a few days or weeks are nothing to worry about. After all, the bank is charging interest on the overdue payments."
- "If I do not have money to repay a loan, I can always borrow more!"

Recognizing one's mistakes and accepting the need to work towards greater credit awareness is perhaps the first and foremost step in steering out of a default situation.

Take Corrective Action

Recognizing credit mistakes is important. However, it has to be combined with concrete steps towards corrective action. This boils down to making sacrifices, cutting out non-essential expenses and paying the creditors their dues.

Taking corrective action would also involve planning. A 3 step program is recommended in order to be able to achieve the desired objectives.

a) Learn to budget
b) Draw an action plan/ Take corrective action
c) Stick to the plan

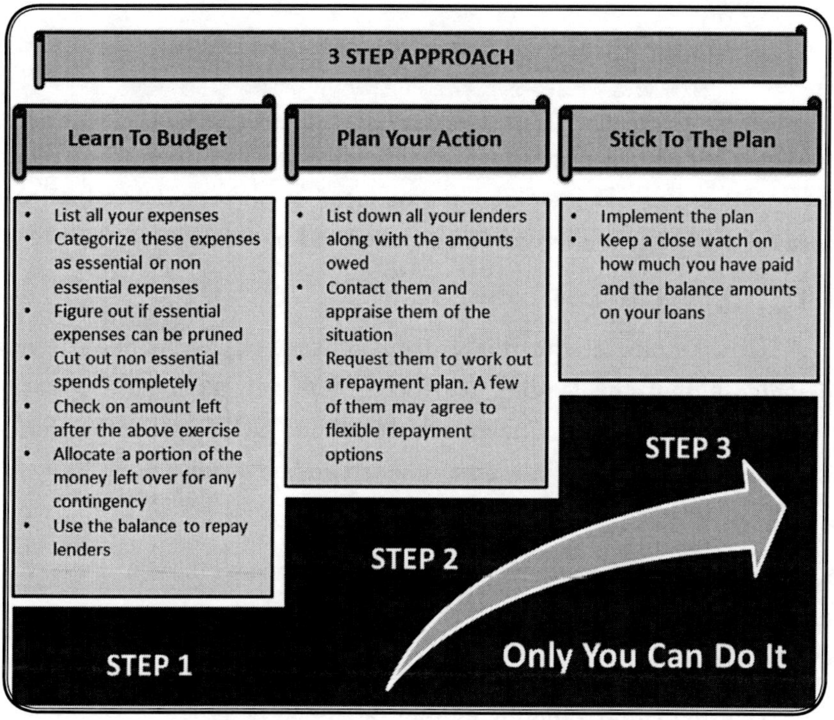

Taking Corrective Action: A 3 Step Approach

In this context, it is important to note that even those who have "settled" and "zeroised" (the outstanding on the credit report is updated as zero) their accounts, have to work with the lending institutions to make good on the waivers that were offered during the settlement. The settlement amount is an amount that both the lender and borrower agree upon for the closure of the account. However, the reality is that since the borrower has not paid the complete amount, the lender has incurred losses on this transaction. These accounts are reported to the credit bureaus by the lending institutions as "SETTLED" accounts. Such settled accounts have a negative impact on a person's credit profile.

Thus, even those who have settled a default are likely to have to pay back to the bank.

Settling an overdue account does not improve your credit profile. As a matter of fact, a "settlement" represents a negative remark on a credit report and adversely impacts the credit underwriting decision.

Flags on a Bureau Report

Every account on a credit report is associated with a FLAG which denotes its current status. These flags are updated by the reporting institution based on a pre-agreed list of flags (specified by the RBI)

- DPD (Days Past Due)

  A "000" indicates that there are no missed payments and a * would indicate that the lending institution has not reported the account in that month. Any number greater than "000" indicates that the payments have been missed by those number of days
- Standard

  Indicates that the payments have been made within 90 days of the due date
- NPA (Non-performing Asset)

  Any account that remains unpaid for 90 days gets marked as a non-performing asset (NPA)
- SUB (Sub Standard)

  An account that continues to be NPA for a period of 12 months
- Doubtful

  An account that remains SUB (sub-standard) for a period of 12 months
- Settlement

  This status signifies that there was a mutual agreement between the borrower and lending institution. As part of this arrangement, a part of the outstanding on a loan is waived to close the account
- Write off

  A Write off indicates that the lending institution has not been able to collect any outstanding amounts and has marked the account as a loss

- **Post write off settlement**

  This status signifies that there was a mutual agreement with the bank after the account was declared as a loss and a certain amount was waived off against the outstanding to close the account

- **Suit filed**

  Indicates that a legal case is in process between the lending institution and the borrower

- **Willful defaulter**

  Denotes that the borrower has not paid the dues despite having the capability to repay

- **Blank**

  A blank flag generally implies that the account is not in default.

The above is only an indicative list. An exhaustive list of "flags" is available in the annexure (How to read a Credit Report)

Know Your Rights

While every borrower has a responsibility towards the lenders, one must also be aware of the rights that are available to borrowers. All borrowers (irrespective of current default status), are entitled to the following rights:

- Every borrower has a legitimate right to know the details of amounts quoted by lending institutions to normalize the account. Borrowers must ask for an account statement giving details on various components of the closure amount. The statement should capture the principal outstanding, interest charged, late fees and other charges which may have been levied.
- Every borrower has the right to approach the Banking Ombudsman in the event of a dispute. The first level of escalation could be the concerned bank's internal grievance officer. In the event of continued non-resolution, the matter may be further escalated to the Banking Ombudsman appointed by the Reserve Bank of India (RBI).

- Every borrower has the right to raise any dispute with the consumer court, if required. However, one should be cautious in raising only genuine cases with the consumer courts. Any escalation which does not comply with norms might hurt the interests of the borrower (in the form of delayed resolutions and continued accrual of interest charges).
- Every borrower has the right to be treated with respect by the lending institution and its collection agents. Every lending institution has to follow a stipulated Code of Conduct and no deviation from this code is permitted.

More details on this topic are available in the Annexure on the CIC – Credit Information Companies Act 2005

Model Code of Conduct – Collection Agencies*

The Indian Banking Association (IBA) has designed a Model Policy on Collection of Dues. This code applies to all the staff or any person authorized to represent a bank in the process of collection of dues from a customer. The main points of this code are:

1. Customers need to be treated with dignity
2. All calls made to customers must be from recorded lines
3. Customers are entitled to their privacy
4. Customers may be called only between 07:00 hours to 19:00 hours
5. Customer requests that calls/visits to place of work be stopped are to be honored, if he provides a suitable alternate number/ address where he may be reached during stipulated collection working hours

* To read the complete Code of Conduct visit http://www.iba.org.in/events/(c)%20rev%20comp.doc

Ask Your Creditors for a Helping Hand

In the case of a borrower who has defaulted in the past and genuinely desires to work on the improvement of his credit health, lenders may look at extending a few reasonable concessions to him. So long as the intentions are genuine, one should not shy away from asking the lending institutions for a helping hand.

In cases involving large over dues, a lender may be agreeable to a deferred payment plan. What this means is that the borrower might have the flexibility to repay the outstanding amounts over a few months. For example, a person owing an amount of Rs. 100,000 may be able to repay it over 4 months (Rs. 25,000 per month).

Seeking Professional Help

What is a credit repair company?

A credit repair company is an organization which assists consumers with credit counselling, debt settlement, removing inaccuracies from your credit report and works on strategies to build your credit.

When should you approach a credit repair company?

You need the services of a credit repair company :

- If you are very busy and don't have the time or patience to do the legwork involved in contacting the credit bureaus, your creditors and anyone else who could help in restoring and enhancing your credit.
- If your credit situation is very bad and you don't know how to deal with the situation, it might be the right time to head to a professional.

How do I choose the right credit repair company?

- Chose a company which has been in existence for some amount of time (at least 3 years).
- Choose a company which signs a contract with you.
- Avoid companies which make outrageous promises; like improving your credit profile instantly!

In a few cases (especially where the where the loan is secured by an asset), the lender may be willing to evaluate the request for restructuring of the loan. In other words, the lender may (based on factors such as current outstanding, current income and the value of the security) extend the tenure of the loan. This will have the effect of reducing the monthly outflows while keeping the account status "current".

In certain instances, lending institutions may agree to an interest moratorium on the account so that it does not attract any further interest or charges. Once the amount to be paid and the duration of such payment is agreed, no further interest gets accrued. This helps to save interest costs for the borrower at a time when the borrower is struggling to make good on the overdue payments.

Bankruptcy: Is this an Option?

Bankruptcy is a situation where an individual or a company is unable to earn money to service their obligations and the total debts are higher than the total assets. From a legal perspective, bankruptcy can be defined as a situation where an individual (or company) is not in a position to pay off his (its) debts.

In western economies, declaring bankruptcy is viewed as a financial solution focused on repaying debts for people and businesses suffering heavy losses. In India, however, bankruptcy is considered a personal failure and there is considerable stigma associated with this process.

Under the Provisional Insolvency Act, 1920, and The Presidency Towns Insolvency Act, 1908, individuals may approach the courts to file for insolvency. This Act does not apply to companies (experts have indicated that the bankruptcy laws in India are obsolete and need extensive amendments). As of March 2015, the government is proposing to implement a new comprehensive bankruptcy code which will make it easier for entrepreneurs to exit unviable ventures along the lines of norms prevailing in developed economies.

Filing bankruptcy has both advantages and disadvantages:

Pros:

1. Bankruptcy helps to focus on efforts to rebuild and start life on a fresh note. Once bankruptcy has been filed, all the lenders can be directed to the court receiver.

Cons:

1. The person filing for bankruptcy loses all his assets.
2. Bankruptcy is associated with stigma in the Indian context.

Key Points

- Ineffective management of funds and the lack of credit literacy are the main reasons that lead to default situations
- Recognize your mistakes and then take corrective action
- Live within your means : money saved is money earned
- Know your rights as a borrower
- Do not "SETTLE" with lending institutions. It will hurt your credit. Instead, ask the lending institutions for a helping hand and work towards a clean bureau track record

TIP-IV

Use your Credit Wisely

Credit: A double-edged sword

Credit is a double edged sword. On the one hand, it can help to fulfil our needs and aspirations. On the other hand, when not handled properly, it can damage our finances severely. Therefore, it becomes very important to manage our credit wisely and not fall into debt traps.

The inability to use credit properly and a limited understanding of how credit functions are major gaps in India. People fall into credit traps most commonly on account of credit card usage. When used wisely, a credit card offers a flexible mode of payment along with the convenience of being able to track all our transactions. However, the same credit card could degenerate into a never ending cycle of interest charges and minimum payments, when used in a reckless manner.

Krishna R

Krishna R has a monthly salary of Rs. 50,000. He decided to buy a high end LED TV during the Diwali festival. He bought one with a price tag of Rs. 50,000 using his credit card. This was the first time he was buying a high value product on his credit card in the last 10 years. Thus far, Krishna had been using his credit card only to pay his utility bills online and was paying his monthly outstanding in full before the due date. With the purchase of the TV, Krishna started to pay the minimum amount due (5% of Credit Card dues) every month.

What Krishna did not know was the following:

- The minimum payment due of 5% is only a "minimum" basic requirement. Any amount over and above the minimum amount can be paid to reduce the total outstanding.

- Krishna does not need to wait for the due date to pay the dues to the bank. He has the flexibility to pay any amount that he can spare on any day of the month.
- The interest is charged on a daily outstanding balance. In other words, interest is charged on the outstanding balance on a daily basis and added to the total outstanding. The next day's interest is calculated on this revised outstanding.
- Because Krishna revolves on the credit card balance (pays only 5% of the dues), any fresh purchase accrues interest from the date of the purchase and no free credit period (as is the case normally) is available to the client. This manner of interest calculation is normal for credit card companies.
- Any payment made by Krishna gets adjusted firstly against interest and charges (such as late fees) and the remainder gets adjusted against the principal outstanding.

The following illustration gives us an idea of how revolving (paying only 5% of monthly dues) on a credit card can impact the financials of an individual:

Illustration

It takes 105 months to pay an amount of Rs. 50,000 if only 5% (minimum amount due) is paid every month!

Let us assume that a credit card is used for Rs. 50,000. The card holder will take almost 9 years to pay off the dues (subject to the card not being utilized again in these 9 years). This is because of the high rate of interest (normally upwards of 36% per annum) which is charged on the card. Paying 5% of the dues every month barely covers the interest which is levied every month.

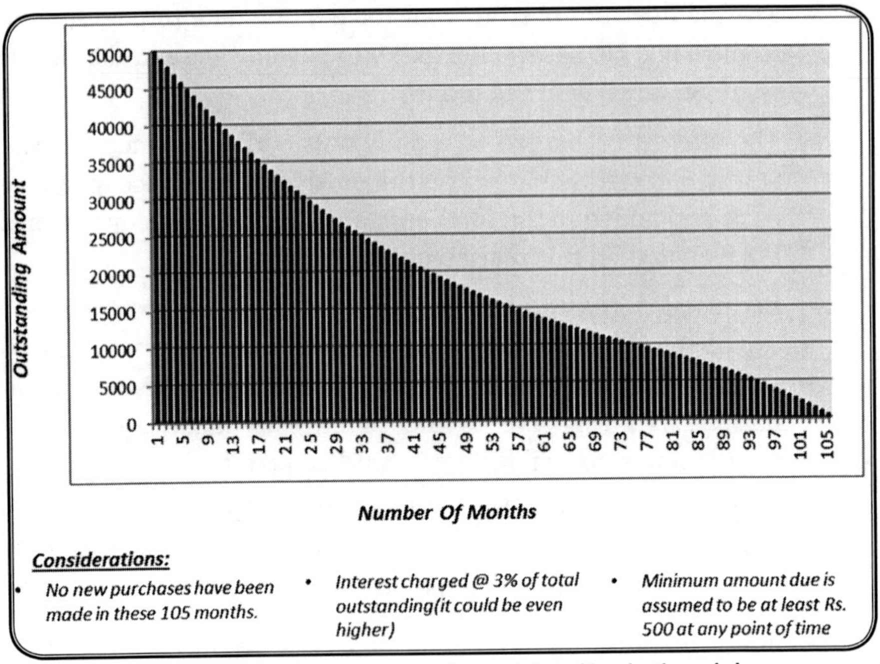

Number of months required to repay credit card debt if only the minimum amount due is paid every month

In Krishna's case, he has chosen to pay the minimum amount due every month. By our calculations, he will have to pay Rs. 61,826 as interest on account of the purchase that he has made (Rs. 50,000) on his credit card !

Individuals need to exercise considerable caution while managing credit. The following facts ought to be kept in mind:

◈ Pay Your Dues on Time

Paying your dues in time (preferably earlier than the due date) is of utmost importance to maintain a good credit score. Any delays can impact an individual's credit score negatively. Payment history is a key factor in determining credit scores. Paying in time keeps one on the right side of the credit bureau and also helps in avoiding additional charges from getting levied on your accounts. Set reminders on all your payments. Also, as far as possible, pay your credit card dues in full (avoid paying only the minimum amount due).

Good Credit v/s Bad Credit

The following are some forms of "Good Credit"

- Credit to finance education
- Credit used to buy a house, especially when used for self-occupation
- Credit used to expand a business and its profitability

The following are some forms of "Bad Credit"

- Credit used to finance consumptions items such as expensive clothes, luxury holidays and other non-essential items
- Credit card usage where one is unable to pay off the full outstanding before the due date
- Credit used to finance speculation such as stock market investments and gambling

---

- Do not over expose yourself to Credit

  While credit helps us to achieve our financial objectives, over exposure to it could cause us to tip over into a debt trap! Consumers should know the difference between good credit and bad credit so that they can avoid the bad forms and benefit from the good forms of credit.

- Stay well within your credit limits

  The credit limit is the maximum permissible amount that an individual may use on his credit card. It is not advisable to use more than 40 % of your credit limit at any given point of time. Higher usage of the credit limit not only exposes you to the risk of not being able to pay the outstanding amount in full but also has a negative impact on your credit score.

- Keep track of all your loans and their balances

  It is important to keep track of all your loans and their outstanding. Do keep a log starting from the month of inception of your credit facilities and track these through to their complete repayment. Review the log every month so that you are able to plan for the payments and do not miss out on the due date for any of your credit facilities.

Various online tools are available that can help you to keep track and remind you on all your recurring payments. You can subscribe to one of them in case you are using a smart phone and are comfortable using mobile applications.

- Avoid reducing the amount of your monthly EMI

  Many a times, it has been observed that when interest rates get revised downward, the borrower puts up a request to the lending institution for a reduction in the EMI. This should be avoided given the fact that in any loan with a long tenure, the interest component forms the larger part of the EMI (Equated Monthly Instalment) in the initial years. Therefore, any reduction in the EMI has a bearing on your final payout to the bank. On the contrary, if you continue to pay the same EMI, the additional money helps to reduce your principal outstanding and enables you to repay your loan faster.

- Increase your EMI when you can

  In the event of an increase in your salary or getting a bonus, one should try to increase the EMI (especially if you have an active home loan). It would be even better to pay off a lump sum amount to reduce your loan outstanding. This helps to reduce the principal outstanding on the loan, repay your loan faster and save interest costs.

- Avoid multiple inquiries for the same credit facility

  An inquiry is the result of a lending institution querying the bureau database for your credit report so that it may assess your credit character while deciding on your loan application. Multiple inquiries are reflective of credit hunger and are detrimental to your credit score. Often direct sales agents (DSAs), pass on your credit application to multiple banks to maximize the chances of approval of the credit facility.

- Avoid being a co borrower on a loan

  One should avoid being a co borrower on a credit facility, unless it is essential. This is especially true when you are a co-borrower on a loan with unrelated individuals. One should note that that not only do these loans reflect in your bureau report, but also that, as a co borrower you are liable for all of the outstanding dues in the event of default by the borrower.

- Avoid being a Guarantor to a credit facility

  Being a guarantor on a loan entails as much risk as being a borrower of the loan. Decisions to be a guarantor are primarily based on personal relationships and the assumption that the person, for whom the guarantee is being provided, will repay the loan. However, that may not always be the case. The guarantor is liable to pay the overdue amount in case the primary applicant is unable to meet the repayment obligations. Also, the loan reflects on the credit report of guarantor and impacts the guarantor's credit score negatively, in the event of any default by the borrower.

- Do not close your active accounts

  Do not close your active accounts since this can be detrimental to your credit health. The length of a credit account impacts the credit score. Hence, in case there is a credit facility that you have been using for a few years, do not close it. Instead, use it wisely!

Key Points

- Credit gives us access to a world of conveniences: it should be used responsibly
- Try to pay your credit card dues in full. It takes 105 months to pay off an outstanding of Rs. 50,000 on a credit card if the card holder pays only the minimum amount due every month
- Your bank account should be funded before the EMI due date and in the case of a credit card, the payment must be made before the due date
- Set reminders for all your payments to avoid missing out on due dates
- Being a co-borrower or guarantor carries the same risk as taking a loan in your own name (the guarantor carries the risk in the event of default by the person on whose behalf the guarantee is made). It is prudent to avoid being a co borrower or guarantor unless it is essential
- Do not close your active accounts. The higher the vintage of the accounts in your credit portfolio, the better your credit score is likely to be
- Do not overuse your credit cards. Do ensure that the usage on your credit card is no more than 40% of your credit limit

TIP-V

Keep your Credit Protected

Your Credit is precious and needs to be kept protected for a lifetime. While building your credit profile may take considerable efforts, a few rash steps are enough to wreak havoc on your financial life.

Although there is an intrinsic need to keep one's credit protected, very few people are aware of the steps that they need to take to keep themselves covered against the perils that could hurt their credit profile.

The key risks to any an individual's credit profile are:

- Credit traps
- Credit related frauds

Credit Traps

A debt or credit trap is a situation in which an individual borrows money, but does not have enough money to make the interest payments on his loan. The individual takes another loan to make the interest payments and to cover the first loan's payments. This creates a vicious cycle where the individual is likely to have to borrow again to pay off the second loan.

There are some simple steps that one could take in order to avoid falling into such situations.

Common Credit Traps in India

- **Credit Illiteracy: Not Reading the Fine Print**
  Most of India is relatively new to organized retail credit. Often, loan agreements are signed without reading the fine print. The lack of awareness of loan terms and conditions, interest rates, loan tenure and the consequences of default are common reasons for debt spiraling out of control.

- **Speculating on Indian Real Estate**
  Rising home prices in urban India over the last decade have encouraged speculation on real estate transactions. These have been spurred on by attractive schemes from builders (buy now, pay later structures).With stagnating home prices, falling rental yields and high maintenance costs, the possibility of being "stuck" with a nonproductive asset is a risk that all real estate speculators should contend with.

- **Not having enough Insurance**
  The low average age of Indians combined with limited awareness of the benefits of insurance have meant that most people in India (even in urban areas) are underinsured. This means that they have a limited ability to weather the costs of the various uncertainties that could derail their income and expense budgets.

- **Mismanaging credit card expenses**
  The authors have observed that many people revolve (pay 5% of their dues) on their card dues. This often leads to a vicious cycle of mounting interest payments and increased dues on their credit cards.

Prepare a budget

The most common reason for falling into a debt trap is one's inability to curtail expenses. As the first step, one needs to prepare a budget.

The budgeting exercise usually covers the following steps:

- Collate all incomes (including rental and other income sources such as the interest that you may earn on your savings account).
- Draw a list of all your expenses and separate them into essential and non-essential categories (essential expenses are the ones that are needed for survival; such as food, medical and rental expenses). Non-essential expenses are the ones where the buying decision could either be deferred or done away with completely; such as eating out frequently and luxury holidays. Check on the percentage of your income getting spent on each of these segments.
- Make a plan to see how you can bring down the share of non-essential expenses.
- Review the budget every month and make changes as required.
- Endeavour to stick to the budget.

To be able to effectively plan your budget, you may use any one of the various tools and spreadsheets available online (for free). We have also provided an indicative budgeting sheet as a starting point (refer to annexure II). You may want to use the tool in its current format or may desire to modify it to suit your requirements.

Money Savers

Every rupee saved is a rupee earned. Therefore, it is advisable to be smart about planning expenses. There are hundreds of items on which we can save a lot of money if these purchases are planned properly.

PRACTICAL MONEY SAVERS

- Purchasing items in a sale can help to bring down the costs to a considerable extent
- Pooling a car and sharing the ride with a colleague or using public transport can add to savings
- Restricting telephone discussions can help in bringing down the cost of telephone calls
- Paying only for the required television channels can help in bringing down the cost of a cable connection
- Exercising in the open rather than a gym has the potential of saving at least a couple of thousand rupees every month
- Inculcating the habit of switching off lights and fans in rooms where they are not being used can bring down the electricity bill
- Asking for cheaper options on medicines from doctors can lead to large savings on medical bills
- Carrying lunch to work can bring down your expenses and keep you healthy
- Wash clothes at home rather than give them to a dry cleaner
- Sell items that are not in use (or not likely to get used) but are in your possession

While everyone can benefit from preparing a budget, such "belt tightening" exercises are extremely useful to those who are going through a financial crisis and would like to avoid a debt trap.

Contingency Fund

A contingency fund is an amount kept aside to meet any exigency or emergency situation. Ideally, an individual needs to set aside a minimum of six months of expenses as a contingency fund. This money can be used to pay debts, meet day to day expenses in the event of a business downturn or job loss or even to take care of unexpected medical expenses.

Insurance

Unexpected expenses could easily derail the best of budgeting exercises. Insurance could be a cost effective way to counter some of the uncertainties that life throws at us.

Medical Insurance: Adequate medical insurance could help to cover medical costs in the event of hospitalization.

Home Insurance: Natural calamities (such as floods) arrive without warning and could devastate our homes. Available at a highly affordable premium, home insurance covers the cost of restoring our homes in the event of such calamities.

Motor Insurance: A lot of people in India drive cars and two-wheelers. However, they are largely underinsured (only third party liability coverage of motor insurance is mandated by law). Comprehensive motor insurance covers are highly recommended to ensure a safety net in the event of road accidents.

Credit Frauds

Credit fraud is a wide-ranging term for theft involving the fraudulent usage of a payment device, such as a credit card or debit card. The purpose of a credit fraud is usually to obtain goods without paying for them or to obtain unauthorized funds from an account.

The most common financial frauds are those involving:

- Identity Theft
- Misuse of financial instruments
  - Credit or Debit Card misuse
  - Loss of Credit or Debit Card

The following are some simple steps that could be taken to minimize the risk of such frauds:

Identity Theft

Identity Theft is a crime where a fraudster steals another person's personal information such as his PAN number, Aadhar number or other such personal identifiers in order to impersonate that person. The fraudster then uses the victim's information to obtain credit facilities in the name of the victim or to steal money by impersonating the victim. This leaves the victim reeling under the financial liability of a debt that he did not incur. Sometimes, Identity Theft may even be serious enough to lead to criminal liability for the person whose identity has been stolen.

An individual's personal data could get compromised in two ways:

- Loss of the physical copy of documents such as PAN card, Aadhar Card, bank statements, tax returns, pay slips or other personal identification documents.

India: A Soft Target for Identity Theft

- **As per NCRB (National Crime Record Bureau, the instances of cybercrime and Identity Theft in India are growing at a rate of over 60% on a year on year basis.**
- **The lack of awareness, combined with the lack of knowledge preventive and monitoring tools makes Indians a soft target for Identity Theft.**

Often such documents are handed over to unknown individuals without adequate precautions. This can lead to misuse of such documents leading to identity fraud.

- Most of us have an online presence and share information about ourselves and our families on various social platforms such as Facebook, Twitter, and Google+ among others. We are also active on E mails and "Chat" accounts where we share information, sometimes with relatively unknown persons or even strangers. Cyber thieves could illegally access confidential information and use this information to impersonate you and steal money.

The following precautions ought to be taken to protect against Identity Theft.

Guard Physical Documents:

- Copies of identity documents should be handed over to authorized individuals only and should be self-attested with signature, date and purpose.
- Do not handover originals of identity documents to anyone for photocopying.
- Keep your original identification documents in safe custody at all times.
- Do not keep copies of sensitive and important documents in places where they could be misused. Instead, shred unwanted copies at regular intervals.

Guard Online Accounts:

- Secure access to all your online accounts by using complex passwords. Use a password with a minimum of 8 characters. Try to incorporate alphabets, numbers and some special characters to keep cyber thieves at bay.
- Do not disclose your login IDs and passwords to anyone.
- Change the passwords of your online accounts at regular intervals.
- While making an online transaction, ensure that website uses a secure encryption. The website address should begin with https:// ("s" signifies a secured website).
- Be alert on phishing. Phishing is a technique used by scammers to mimic a legitimate website or business to gain access to your personal information. Please be aware that no bank or legitimate business will ask for your personal details (other than when you may be creating a new account with them).

How do you know whether you are the victim of Identity Theft?

You could be a victim of Identity Theft if:

- Your credit bureau report records an account that you are unable to identify as your own.
- The personal information given on your credit bureau report is wrong.
- Your credit bureau report records inquiries that you have not made.
- Your card statement reflects a transaction which you are unable to identify.
- You start to get calls from collection agencies for overdue payments (in spite of not having missed any payments).
- You abruptly stop receiving monthly statements/bills of your credit facilities.

How does one deal with Identity Theft?

Act Immediately

If you suspect that you are the victim of Identity Theft, please do the following immediately:

- Call up the concerned financial institution immediately and inform them about the suspected Identity Theft. Document the conversation with an E mail to the lending institution.
- Discontinue the credit or debit card which may have been exposed to Identity Theft.
- If you suspect that your online passwords may have been compromised, change the passwords of all your accounts without delay.
- Victims of Identity Theft should lodge a formal complaint with the local cyber-crime cell of the police department.

"Identity Theft" is one of the fastest growing crimes in world. As per the Norton Cyber Crime Report, over 55 crore individuals' identities got exposed in 2013 which is 493% higher than 2012 figures! The total amount estimated to have been lost on account of exposed identities runs into billions of dollars.

Steps to counter Identity Theft

Credit Monitoring

Credit monitoring is a tool which alerts you with an update as and when there is a change to your credit bureau report. In the event of any new inquiry or other details getting changed, the person who has signed up for the credit monitoring service will immediately get notified. You may sign up for credit monitoring by registering with www.freescoreindia.com.

Identity Theft Insurance

The costs of Identity Theft can be mitigated with an insurance policy which covers the individual against liabilities in the event of identity fraud. Such covers are not readily available to retail customers in the Indian context.

Your credit is precious. Whether is steering clear of debt traps or keeping identity thieves at bay, the onus is clearly on each and every individual to keep their credit protected from these perils which can rob them of this precious virtue!

Key Points

- Your credit is precious. Keep it protected from debt traps and financial frauds
- Credit Traps can be avoided by creating a budget, consciously saving money and planning for contingencies by maintaining a fund
- Create a budget and review it every month. Try to minimize your expenses on non-discretionary items
- Keep a close watch on all your expenses. You may wish to utilize online tools which are readily available for effective tracking
- Financial frauds such as Identity Theft are increasing in frequency in India
- Act immediately if you suspect that you are a victim of Identity Theft
- Be proactive with tools such as credit monitoring to protect yourself from Identity Theft

PART IV

Annexures

ANNEXURE-I

How to Read a Credit Bureau Report

This section attempts to give you a step-by-step approach to decipher your credit report. A credit report may be divided into the following sections:

1. **Score**

   A Credit score is a three digit number that denotes an individual's creditworthiness. In other words, the credit score is a numerical measure of an individual's credit character.

2. **Personal Details**

   - Name/DOB/Gender
   - All addresses, office and residence, that have been reported
   - All contact numbers
   - Email IDs
   - Government ID details that have been given to banks/ financial institutions

3. **Account Details**

   - Type of loan
   - Account Number
   - Bank/Lander Name
   - Loan Amount
   - Current Balance
   - Start Date
   - Close Date (if already closed)
   - Current Status (Open/Closed/Written Off/Settled etc.)
   - Repayment history for last 36 months

4. Inquiries

- List of all banks/lending institutions requesting for data on an individual
- Product inquired for
- Amount applied for

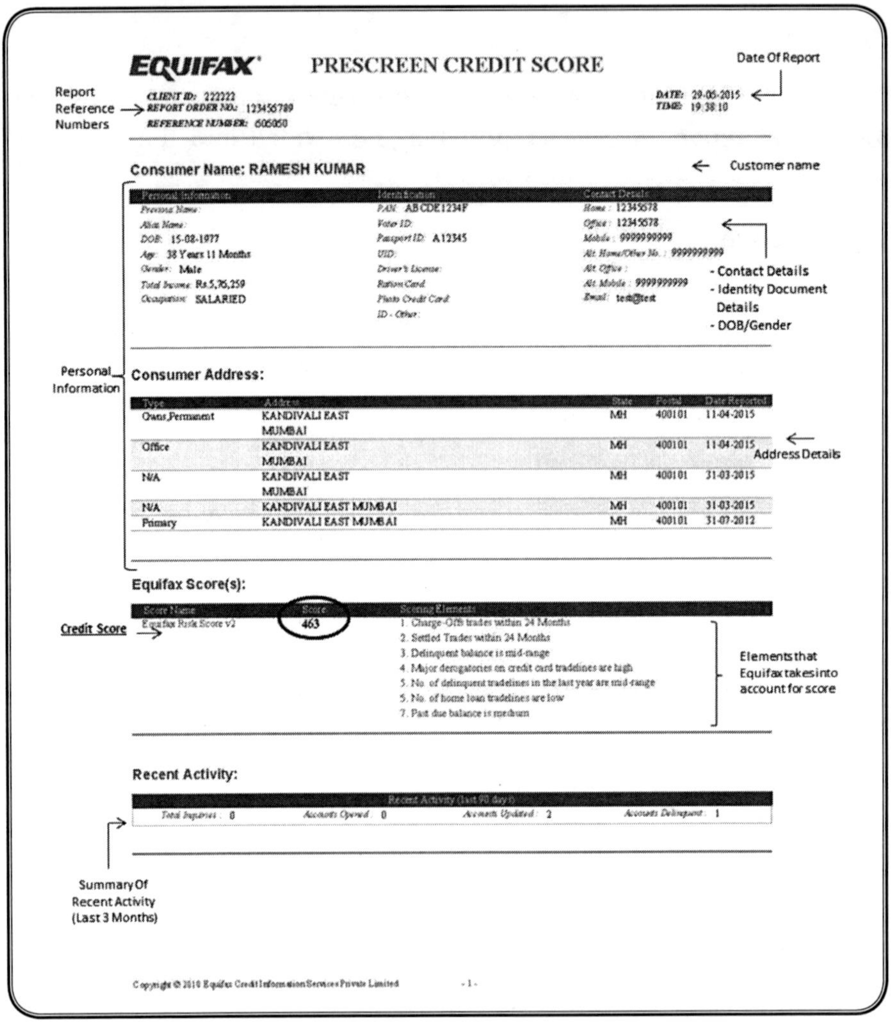

EQUIFAX PRESCREEN CREDIT SCORE

CLIENT ID: 222222
REPORT ORDER NO: 123456789
REFERENCE NUMBER: 606060

DATE: 29-06-2015
TIME: 19:38:10

Consumer Name: RAMESH KUMAR

Personal Information	Identification	Contact Details
Previous Name:	PAN: ABCDE1234F	Home: 12345678
Alias Name:	Voter ID:	Office: 12345678
DOB: 15-08-1977	Passport ID: A12345	Mobile: 9999999999
Age: 38 Years 11 Months	UID:	Alt. Home/Other No.: 9999999999
Gender: Male	Driver's License:	Alt. Office:
Total Income: Rs.5,76,259	Ration Card:	Alt. Mobile: 9999999999
Occupation: SALARIED	Photo Credit Card:	Email: test@test
	ID - Other:	

Consumer Address:

Type	Address	State	Postal	Date Reported
Owns,Permanent	KANDIVALI EAST MUMBAI	MH	400101	11-04-2015
Office	KANDIVALI EAST MUMBAI	MH	400101	11-04-2015
N/A	KANDIVALI EAST MUMBAI	MH	400101	31-03-2015
N/A	KANDIVALI EAST MUMBAI	MH	400101	31-03-2015
Primary	KANDIVALI EAST MUMBAI	MH	400101	31-07-2012

Equifax Score(s):

Score Name	Score	Scoring Elements
Equifax Risk Score v2	463	1. Charge-Offs trades within 24 Months 2. Settled Trades within 24 Months 3. Delinquent balance is mid-range 4. Major derogatories on credit card tradelines are high 5. No. of delinquent tradelines in the last year are mid-range 5. No. of home loan tradelines are low 7. Past due balance is medium

Recent Activity:

Recent Activity (last 90 days)			
Total Inquiries: 0	Accounts Opened: 0	Accounts Updated: 2	Accounts Delinquent: 1

Copyright © 2010 Equifax Credit Information Services Private Limited -1-

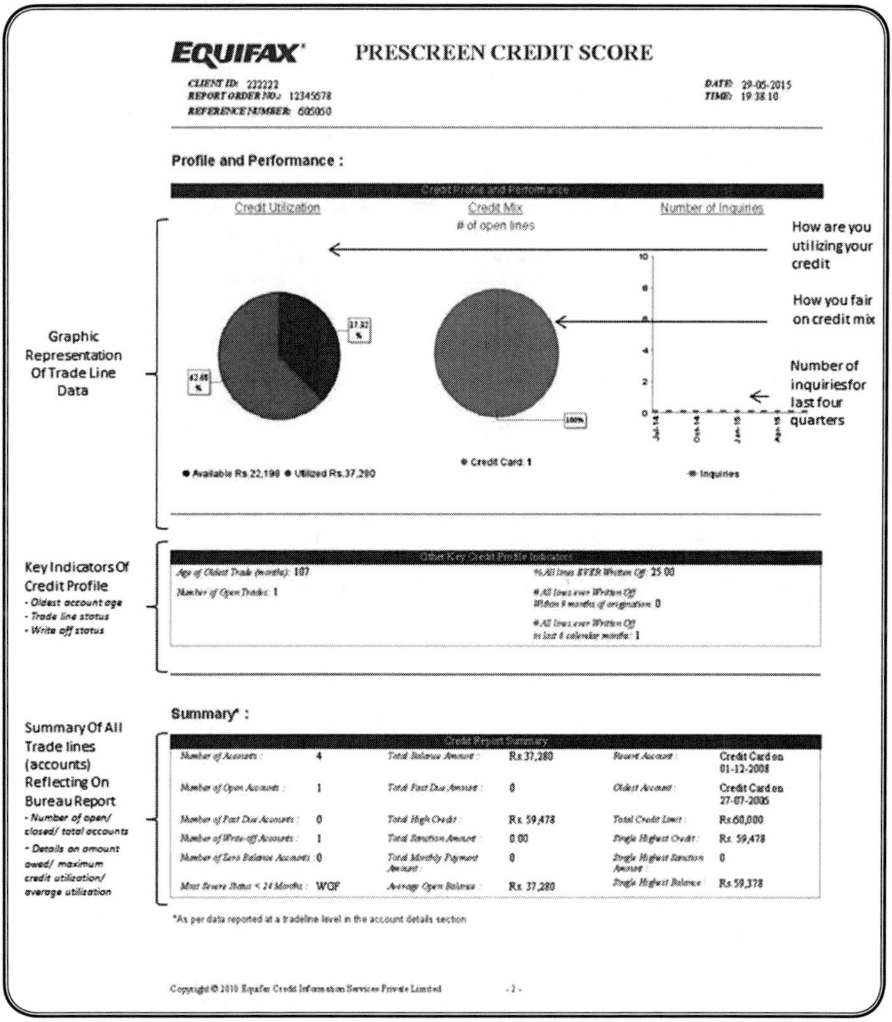

EQUIFAX®   PRESCREEN CREDIT SCORE

CLIENT ID: 222222
REPORT ORDER NO.: 12345678
REFERENCE NUMBER: 606060

DATE: 29-05-2015
TIME: 19:38:10

Profile and Performance :

Credit Profile and Performance

Key Indicators Of Credit Profile
- *Oldest account age*
- *Trade line status*
- *Write off status*

Other Key Credit Profile Indicators	
Age of Oldest Trade (months): 107	*%All lines EVER Written Off:* 25.00
Number of Open Trades: 1	*#All lines ever Written Off Within 6 months of origination:* 0
	#All lines ever Written Off in last 6 calendar months: 1

Summary* :

Summary Of All Trade lines (accounts) Reflecting On Bureau Report
- *Number of open/ closed/ total accounts*
- *Details on amount owed/ maximum credit utilization/ average utilization*

Credit Report Summary					
Number of Accounts :	4	*Total Balance Amount :*	Rs.37,280	*Recent Account :*	Credit Card on 01-12-2008
Number of Open Accounts :	1	*Total Past Due Amount :*	0	*Oldest Account :*	Credit Card on 27-07-2006
Number of Past Due Accounts :	0	*Total High Credit :*	Rs. 59,478	*Total Credit Limit :*	Rs.60,000
Number of Write-off Accounts :	1	*Total Sanction Amount :*	0.00	*Single Highest Credit :*	Rs. 59,478
Number of Zero Balance Accounts :	0	*Total Monthly Payment Amount :*	0	*Single Highest Sanction Amount :*	0
Most Severe Status < 24 Months :	WOF	*Average Open Balance :*	Rs. 37,280	*Single Highest Balance :*	Rs.59,378

*As per data reported at a tradeline level in the account details section

  - 2 -

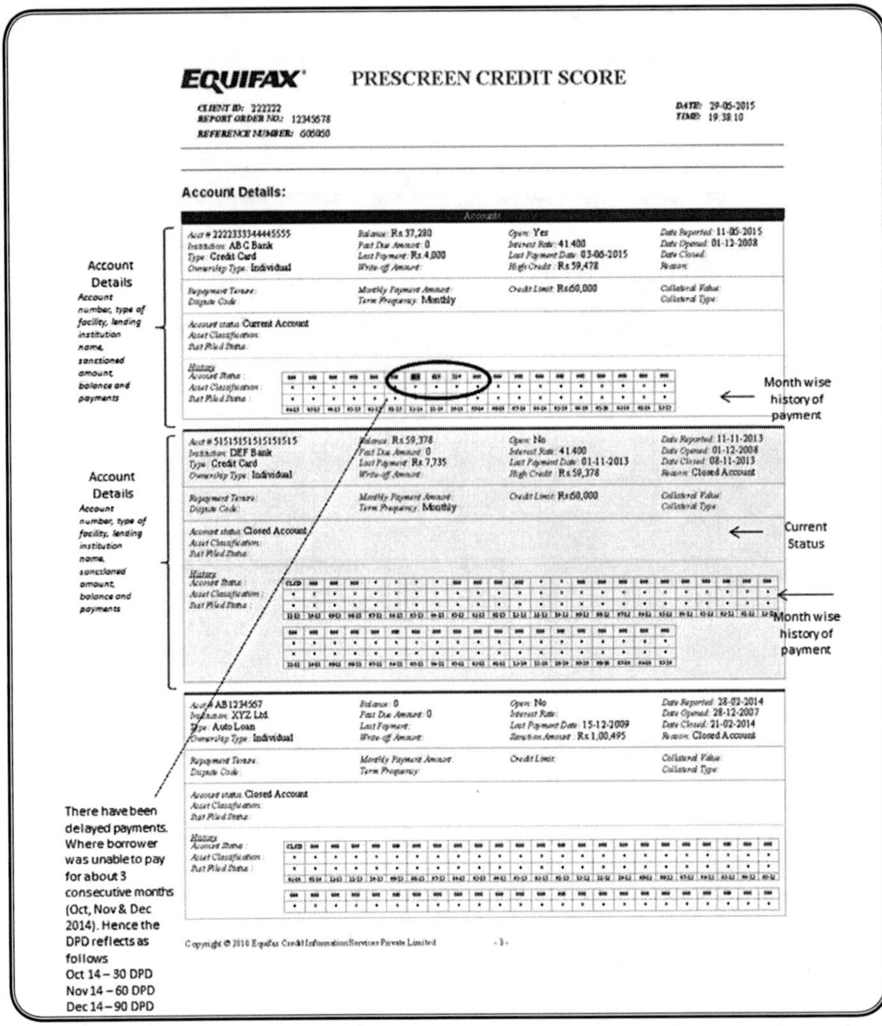

EQUIFAX PRESCREEN CREDIT SCORE

CLIENT ID: 222222
REPORT ORDER NO: 12345678
REFERENCE NUMBER: 606050

DATE: 29-05-2015
TIME: 19:38:10

Account Details:

Accounts

Acct # 2222333344445555	*Balance:* Rs.37,280	*Open:* Yes	*Date Reported:* 11-05-2015
Institution: ABC Bank	*Past Due Amount:* 0	*Interest Rate:* 41.400	*Date Opened:* 01-12-2008
Type: Credit Card	*Last Payment:* Rs.4,000	*Last Payment Date:* 03-06-2015	*Date Closed:*
Ownership Type: Individual	*Write-off Amount:*	*High Credit:* Rs.59,478	*Reason:*
Repayment Tenure:	*Monthly Payment Amount:*	*Credit Limit:* Rs.60,000	*Collateral Value:*
Dispute Code:	*Term Frequency:* Monthly		*Collateral Type:*

Account status: Current Account
Asset Classification:
Suit Filed Status:

History
Account Status:
Asset Classification:
Suit Filed Status:

Acct # 5151515151515151515	*Balance:* Rs.59,378	*Open:* No	*Date Reported:* 11-11-2013
Institution: DEF Bank	*Past Due Amount:* 0	*Interest Rate:* 41.400	*Date Opened:* 01-12-2008
Type: Credit Card	*Last Payment:* Rs.7,735	*Last Payment Date:* 01-11-2013	*Date Closed:* 08-11-2013
Ownership Type: Individual	*Write-off Amount:*	*High Credit:* Rs.59,378	*Reason:* Closed Account
Repayment Tenure:	*Monthly Payment Amount:*	*Credit Limit:* Rs.60,000	*Collateral Value:*
Dispute Code:	*Term Frequency:* Monthly		*Collateral Type:*

Account status: Closed Account
Asset Classification:
Suit Filed Status:

History
Account Status:
Asset Classification:
Suit Filed Status:

Acct # AB1234567	*Balance:* 0	*Open:* No	*Date Reported:* 28-02-2014
Institution: XYZ Ltd.	*Past Due Amount:* 0	*Interest Rate:*	*Date Opened:* 28-12-2007
Type: Auto Loan	*Last Payment:*	*Last Payment Date:* 15-12-2009	*Date Closed:* 21-02-2014
Ownership Type: Individual	*Write-off Amount:*	*Sanction Amount:* Rs.1,00,495	*Reason:* Closed Account
Repayment Tenure:	*Monthly Payment Amount:*	*Credit Limit:*	*Collateral Value:*
Dispute Code:	*Term Frequency:*		*Collateral Type:*

Account status: Closed Account
Asset Classification:
Suit Filed Status:

History
Account Status:
Asset Classification:
Suit Filed Status:

Copyright © 2010 Equifax Credit Information Services Private Limited - 3 -

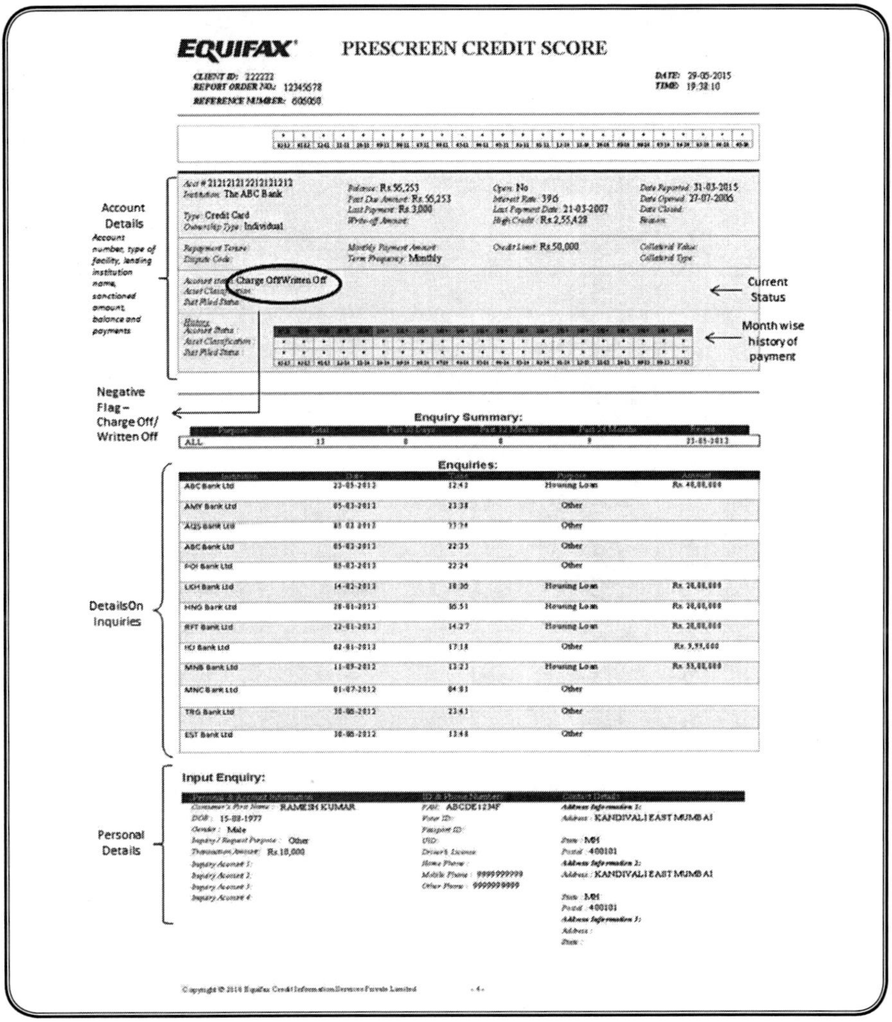

EQUIFAX PRESCREEN CREDIT SCORE

CLIENT ID: 222222
REPORT ORDER NO.: 12345678
REFERENCE NUMBER: 606060
DATE: 29-05-2015
TIME: 19:38:10

Acct # 21212121 2212121212
Institution: The ABC Bank
Type: Credit Card
Ownership Type: Individual
Balance: Rs.56,253
Past Due Amount: Rs.56,253
Last Payment: Rs.3,000
Write-off Amount:
Open: No
Interest Rate: 396
Last Payment Date: 21-03-2007
High Credit: Rs.2,55,428
Date Reported: 31-03-2015
Date Opened: 27-07-2006
Date Closed:
Reason:

Repayment Tenure:
Dispute Code:
Monthly Payment Amount:
Term Frequency: Monthly
Credit Limit: Rs.50,000
Collateral Value:
Collateral Type:

Account status: Charge Off/Written Off
Asset Classification:
Suit Filed Status:

History
Account Status:
Asset Classification:
Suit Filed Status:

Enquiry Summary:

Purpose	Total	Past 30 Days	Past 12 Months	Past 24 Months	Recent
ALL	13	8	8	9	23-05-2013

Enquiries:

Institution	Date	Time	Purpose	Amount
ABC Bank Ltd	23-05-2013	12:43	Housing Loan	Rs. 40,00,000
AMY Bank Ltd	05-03-2013	23:38	Other	
AIZS Bank Ltd	05-03-2013	22:24	Other	
ABC Bank Ltd	05-03-2013	22:35	Other	
FOI Bank Ltd	05-03-2013	22:24	Other	
LKH Bank Ltd	14-02-2013	18:30	Housing Loan	Rs. 20,00,000
HNG Bank Ltd	28-01-2013	16:51	Housing Loan	Rs. 20,00,000
RFT Bank Ltd	22-01-2013	14:27	Housing Loan	Rs. 20,00,000
HJ Bank Ltd	02-01-2013	17:18	Other	Rs. 9,99,000
MNB Bank Ltd	11-09-2012	13:23	Housing Loan	Rs. 55,00,000
MNC Bank Ltd	01-07-2012	04:01	Other	
TRG Bank Ltd	30-05-2012	23:41	Other	
EST Bank Ltd	30-05-2012	13:48	Other	

Input Enquiry:

Personal & Account Information
Consumer's First Name: RAMESH KUMAR
DOB: 15-08-1977
Gender: Male
Inquiry / Request Purpose: Other
Transaction Amount: Rs.10,000
Inquiry Account 1:
Inquiry Account 2:
Inquiry Account 3:
Inquiry Account 4:

ID & Phone Numbers
PAN: ABCDE1234F
Voter ID:
Passport ID:
UID:
Driver's License:
Home Phone:
Mobile Phone: 9999999999
Other Phone: 9999999999

Contact Details
Address Information 1:
Address: KANDIVALI EAST MUMBAI
State: MH
Postal: 400101
Address Information 2:
Address: KANDIVALI EAST MUMBAI
State: MH
Postal: 400101
Address Information 3:
Address:
State:

 - 4 -

EQUIFAX PRESCREEN CREDIT SCORE

CLIENT ID: 222222
REPORT ORDER NO.: 12345678
REFERENCE NUMBER: 605050

DATE: 29-06-2015
TIME: 19:38:10

Postal :

Explanation on Terms and Glossary used

Glossary, Terms and Explanations:

History

Code	Description
000	current account
CLSD	Paid or closed account/zero balance
NEW	New Account
LNSB	Loan Submitted
LAND	Loan Approved - Not yet disbursed
INAC	Account is Inactive
CON	Contact Member for Status
01+	1-30 days past due
31+	31-60 days past due
DEC	Loan Declined
61+	61-90 days past due
SPM	Special Mention
SUB	Sub-standard
RES	Restructured Loan
RGM	Restructured Loan - Govt Mandate
SET	Settled
SF	Suit Filed
91+	91-120 days past due
121+	121 - 179 days past due
181+	180 or more days past due
DBT	Doubtful
FPD	First Payment Default
WDF	Willful Default
PWOS	Post Written Off Settled
WOF	Charge Off/Written Off
STD	Standard
SUB	Sub-standard
DBT	Doubtful
LOSS	Loss
SPM	Special Mention Account
SFR	Suit Filed-Restructured
SF	Suit Filed
WDF	Willful Default
SFWD	Suit Filed-Willful Default
WOF	Written Off
SFWO	Suit Filed and Written Off
WDWO	Willful Default and Written Off
SWDW	Suit Filed, Willful Default and Written Off
SET	Settled
*	Data Not Reported

Contact Us: Phone: 1800 209 3247 Fax: +91-22-6112-7960 Email: ecissupport@equifaxindia.com

 - 5 -

Sample Credit Report - CIBIL

Control No = Customer reference no

CIBIL CREDIT INFORMATION REPORT

Credit Information Bureau (India) Limited
IN ASSOCIATION WITH DUN & BRADSTREET AND TRANSUNION

Date Of Report → DATE: 23-06-2015

CONTROL NUMBER: 123,123,123

INDICATES SECTION IS UNDER DISPUTE

Any dispute shall be indicated by RED Color (*Disputes may be the result of erroneous reporting by LI or algorithm issue at CIC*)

CIBIL TRANSUNION SCORE

Credit Score →

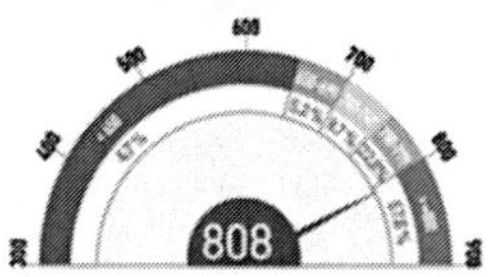

- Your Score
- Figures indicate % of all new loans sanctioned during last 1 years falling in this score band

PERSONAL INFORMATION

Personal Information

NAME	DATE OF BIRTH	GENDER
RAMESH KUMR	15-08-1977	MALE

IDENTIFICATION TYPE	NUMBER	ISSUE DATE	EXPIRATION DATE
INCOME TAX ID NUMBER (PAN)	ABCDE1234F	-	-

CONTACT INFORMATION

All Contact Information furnished by customer

ADDRESS1	CATEGORY	STATUS	DATE REPORTED
KANDIVALI EAST 400101 KANDIVALI EAST 400101 KANDIVALI EAST 400101 MAHARASHTRA-400101	NOT CATEGORIZED	-	21-12-2014

ADDRESS2	CATEGORY	STATUS	DATE REPORTED
KANDIVALI EAST 400101 KANDIVALI EAST 400101 MUMBAI MAHARASHTRA-400101	NOT CATEGORIZED	-	21-12-2014

ADDRESS3	CATEGORY	STATUS	DATE REPORTED
KANDIVALI EAST 400101 MAHARASHTRA-400101	RESIDENCE ADDRESS	-	18-12-2014

ADDRESS4	CATEGORY	STATUS	DATE REPORTED
KANDIVALI EAST 400101 MAHARASHTRA-400101	RESIDENCE ADDRESS	-	17-12-2014

TELEPHONE NUMBERS

TYPE	TELEPHONE NUMBER	EXTENSION
OFFICE PHONE	12345678	713

For more information, please visit our website at www.cibil.com. To log a Dispute, please visit www.cibil.com/dispute/disputeresolution.htm

Page 1 of 13

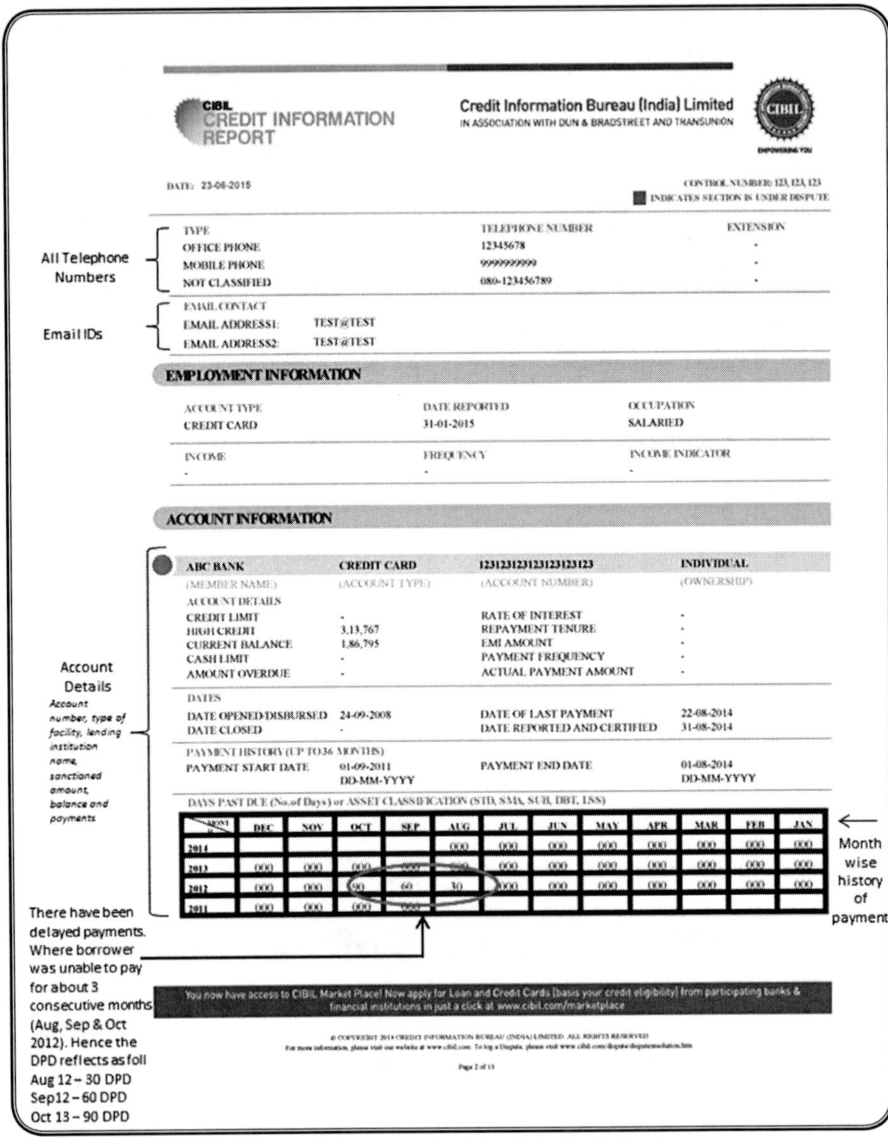

CIBIL
CREDIT INFORMATION REPORT

Credit Information Bureau (India) Limited
IN ASSOCIATION WITH DUN & BRADSTREET AND TRANSUNION

DATE: 23-06-2015

CONTROL NUMBER: 123,123,123
INDICATES SECTION IS UNDER DISPUTE

All Telephone Numbers

TYPE	TELEPHONE NUMBER	EXTENSION
OFFICE PHONE	12345678	-
MOBILE PHONE	9999999999	-
NOT CLASSIFIED	080-123456789	-

Email IDs

EMAIL CONTACT
EMAIL ADDRESS1: TEST@TEST
EMAIL ADDRESS2: TEST@TEST

EMPLOYMENT INFORMATION

ACCOUNT TYPE	DATE REPORTED	OCCUPATION
CREDIT CARD	31-01-2015	SALARIED

INCOME	FREQUENCY	INCOME INDICATOR
-	-	-

ACCOUNT INFORMATION

Account Details
Account number, type of facility, lending institution name, sanctioned amount, balance and payments

ABC BANK	CREDIT CARD	123123123123123123123	INDIVIDUAL
(MEMBER NAME)	(ACCOUNT TYPE)	(ACCOUNT NUMBER)	(OWNERSHIP)

ACCOUNT DETAILS

CREDIT LIMIT	-	RATE OF INTEREST	-
HIGH CREDIT	3,13,767	REPAYMENT TENURE	-
CURRENT BALANCE	1,86,795	EMI AMOUNT	-
CASH LIMIT	-	PAYMENT FREQUENCY	-
AMOUNT OVERDUE	-	ACTUAL PAYMENT AMOUNT	-

DATES

DATE OPENED/DISBURSED	24-09-2008	DATE OF LAST PAYMENT	22-08-2014
DATE CLOSED	-	DATE REPORTED AND CERTIFIED	31-08-2014

PAYMENT HISTORY (UP TO 36 MONTHS)

PAYMENT START DATE	01-09-2011 DD-MM-YYYY	PAYMENT END DATE	01-08-2014 DD-MM-YYYY

DAYS PAST DUE (No.of Days) or ASSET CLASSIFICATION (STD, SMA, SUB, DBT, LSS)

MONTH / YEAR	DEC	NOV	OCT	SEP	AUG	JUL	JUN	MAY	APR	MAR	FEB	JAN
2014					000	000	000	000	000	000	000	000
2013	000	000	000	000	000	000	000	000	000	000	000	000
2012	000	000	90	60	30	000	000	000	000	000	000	000
2011	000	000	000	000								

Month wise history of payment

There have been delayed payments. Where borrower was unable to pay for about 3 consecutive months (Aug, Sep & Oct 2012). Hence the DPD reflects as foll
Aug 12 – 30 DPD
Sep12 – 60 DPD
Oct 13 – 90 DPD

You now have access to CIBIL Market Place! Now apply for Loan and Credit Cards [basis your credit eligibility] from participating banks & financial institutions in just a click at www.cibil.com/marketplace

© COPYRIGHT 2014 CREDIT INFORMATION BUREAU (INDIA) LIMITED. ALL RIGHTS RESERVED
For more information, please visit our website at www.cibil.com. To log a Dispute, please visit www.cibil.com/dispute/disputeresolution.htm

Page 2 of 13

CIBIL CREDIT INFORMATION REPORT

Credit Information Bureau (India) Limited
IN ASSOCIATION WITH DUN & BRADSTREET AND TRANSUNION

DATE: 23-06-2015

CONTROL NUMBER: 123,123,123

INDICATES SECTION IS UNDER DISPUTE

PAYMENT HISTORY (UP TO 36 MONTHS)

PAYMENT START DATE	01-05-2008 DD-MM-YYYY	PAYMENT END DATE	01-05-2010 DD-MM-YYYY

DAYS PAST DUE (No.of Days) or ASSET CLASSIFICATION (STD, SMA, SUB, DBT, LSS)

	DEC	NOV	OCT	SEP	AUG	JUL	JUN	MAY	APR	MAR	FEB	JAN
2010								000	000	000	000	000
2009	000	000	000	000	000	000	000	000	000	000	000	000
2008	000	STD	STD	STD	STD	STD	STD	STD				

COLLATERAL		DEFAULT STATUS	
VALUE OF COLLATERAL	-	SUIT FILED/WILFUL DEFAULT	-
TYPE OF COLLATERAL	-	WRITTEN-OFF STATUS	-
		WRITTEN-OFF AMOUNT(TOTAL)	-
		WRITTEN-OFF AMOUNT(PRINCIPAL)	-
		SETTLEMENT AMOUNT	-

XYZ BANK	CREDIT CARD	121212121212121212	INDIVIDUAL
(MEMBER NAME)	(ACCOUNT TYPE)	(ACCOUNT NUMBER)	(OWNERSHIP)

ACCOUNT DETAILS

CREDIT LIMIT	-	RATE OF INTEREST	-
HIGH CREDIT	2,90,987	REPAYMENT TENURE	-
CURRENT BALANCE	0	EMI AMOUNT	-
CASH LIMIT	-	PAYMENT FREQUENCY	-
AMOUNT OVERDUE	-	ACTUAL PAYMENT AMOUNT	-

DATES

DATE OPENED/DISBURSED	22-10-2007	DATE OF LAST PAYMENT	23-07-2010
DATE CLOSED	08-08-2010	DATE REPORTED AND CERTIFIED	28-02-2014

PAYMENT HISTORY (UP TO 36 MONTHS)

PAYMENT START DATE	01-05-2008 DD-MM-YYYY	PAYMENT END DATE	01-08-2010 DD-MM-YYYY

DAYS PAST DUE (No.of Days) or ASSET CLASSIFICATION (STD, SMA, SUB, DBT, LSS)

	DEC	NOV	OCT	SEP	AUG	JUL	JUN	MAY	APR	MAR	FEB	JAN
2010					000	000	000	038	XXX	036	XXX	000
2009	000	XXX	XXX	XXX	000	000	000	128	098	067	069	008
2008	007	008	000	XXX	XXX	006	004	000				

COLLATERAL		DEFAULT STATUS	
VALUE OF COLLATERAL	-	SUIT FILED/WILFUL DEFAULT	-
TYPE OF COLLATERAL	-	WRITTEN-OFF STATUS	SETTLED
		WRITTEN-OFF AMOUNT(TOTAL)	-
		WRITTEN-OFF AMOUNT(PRINCIPAL)	-
		SETTLEMENT AMOUNT	-

Account Details

Account number, type of facility, lending institution name, sanctioned amount, balance and payments

There have been delayed payments. Hence the Days Past Due – DPD of 08,69,67,98,128 days reflect in the report

Negative Flag "settled"

For more information, please visit our website at www.cibil.com. To log a Dispute, please visit www.cibil.com/dispute/disputeresolution.htm

Page 4 of 13

CIBIL
CREDIT INFORMATION REPORT

Credit Information Bureau (India) Limited
IN ASSOCIATION WITH DUN & BRADSTREET AND TRANSUNION

DATE: 23-06-2015

CONTROL NUMBER: 123,123,123
INDICATES SECTION IS UNDER DISPUTE

DAYS PAST DUE (No.of Days) or ASSET CLASSIFICATION (STD, SMA, SUB, DBT, LSS)

	DEC	NOV	OCT	SEP	AUG	JUL	JUN	MAY	APR	MAR	FEB	JAN
2008											XXX	XXX
2007	000	XXX	000	000	000	STD	STD	STD	STD	STD		

COLLATERAL
VALUE OF COLLATERAL -
TYPE OF COLLATERAL -

DEFAULT STATUS
SUIT FILED/WILFUL DEFAULT -
WRITTEN-OFF STATUS -
WRITTEN-OFF AMOUNT(TOTAL) -
WRITTEN-OFF AMOUNT(PRINCIPAL) -
SETTLEMENT AMOUNT -

Account Wise Detail

ABC BANK	CREDIT CARD	123123123123123123123	INDIVIDUAL
(MEMBER NAME)	(ACCOUNT TYPE)	(ACCOUNT NUMBER)	(OWNERSHIP)

ACCOUNT DETAILS

CREDIT LIMIT	-	RATE OF INTEREST	-
HIGH CREDIT	31,129	REPAYMENT TENURE	-
CURRENT BALANCE	0	EMI AMOUNT	-
CASH LIMIT	-	PAYMENT FREQUENCY	-
AMOUNT OVERDUE	-	ACTUAL PAYMENT AMOUNT	-

DATES

DATE OPENED/DISBURSED	26-11-2005	DATE OF LAST PAYMENT	-
DATE CLOSED	07-04-2011	DATE REPORTED AND CERTIFIED	31-05-2011

PAYMENT HISTORY (UP TO 36 MONTHS)

PAYMENT START DATE	01-11-2007 DD-MM-YYYY	PAYMENT END DATE	01-11-2007 DD-MM-YYYY

DAYS PAST DUE (No.of Days) or ASSET CLASSIFICATION (STD, SMA, SUB, DBT, LSS)

	DEC	NOV	OCT	SEP	AUG	JUL	JUN	MAY	APR	MAR	FEB	JAN
2011		XXX	000	000	000	000	000	000	900	900	900	900

COLLATERAL
VALUE OF COLLATERAL -
TYPE OF COLLATERAL -

DEFAULT STATUS
SUIT FILED/WILFUL DEFAULT -
WRITTEN-OFF STATUS POST (WO) SETTLED
WRITTEN-OFF AMOUNT(TOTAL) -
WRITTEN-OFF AMOUNT(PRINCIPAL) -
SETTLEMENT AMOUNT -

ENQUIRY INFORMATION

Inquiry Details
- *Inquired by*
- *Inquiry date*
- *Loan applied*
- *Amount applied*

MEMBER NAME	DATE OF ENQUIRY	ENQUIRY PURPOSE	ENQUIRY AMOUNT
ABC BANK	12-02-2015	GOLD LOAN	1,50,000
XYZ LTD	08-01-2015	PERSONAL LOAN	1
DEF BANK	21-12-2014	PERSONAL LOAN	5,00,000
PQR LTD	18-12-2014	PERSONAL LOAN	1

Page 12 of 13

CIBIL CREDIT INFORMATION REPORT

Credit Information Bureau (India) Limited
IN ASSOCIATION WITH DUN & BRADSTREET AND TRANSUNION

DATE: 23-06-2015

CONTROL NUMBER: 123,123,123
INDICATES SECTION IS UNDER DISPUTE

Inquiry Details

ABC BANK	17-12-2014	PERSONAL LOAN	5,00,000
DEF BANK	25-11-2014	CREDIT CARD	1,00,000
PQR LTD	[illegible]	PERSONAL LOAN	1
LMN BANK	09-05-2012	PERSONAL LOAN	3,00,000
PQRCARDS	18-04-2012	CREDIT CARD	50,000
OPQ BANK	06-07-2011	CREDIT CARD	10,000
RST BANK	02-11-2010	PERSONAL LOAN	[illegible]
UVW	30-08-2010	CREDIT CARD	50,000
XYZBANK	18-05-2010	CREDIT CARD	50,000
ABC	17-05-2010	CREDIT CARD	[illegible]
ABC PQR	08-09-2009	PERSONAL LOAN	2,00,000
ABC	26-08-2009	CREDIT CARD	[illegible]
ABCDEF BANK	19-08-2009	CREDIT CARD	10,000
ABC	04-08-2009	CREDIT CARD	50,000
ABC	03-08-2009	CREDIT CARD	50,000
PQRS CARDS	23-07-2009	CREDIT CARD	50,000
PQRS BANK	07-07-2009	PERSONAL LOAN	2,00,000
PQRS	29-05-2009	CREDIT CARD	50,000
PQRS BANK	24-04-2009	OTHER	1,000
PQRS	06-03-2009	CREDIT CARD	50,000
ABCD BANK	09-02-2009	PERSONAL LOAN	5,00,000
XYZBANK	16-09-2008	CREDIT CARD	25,000
XYZ	29-05-2008	CREDIT CARD	50,000
ABCD BANK	03-05-2008	PERSONAL LOAN	1,00,000
XYZCARDS	07-12-2007	CREDIT CARD	50,000
ABCD	21-09-2007	CREDIT CARD	15,000
ABCDEF BANK	20-09-2007	CREDIT CARD	1,00,000
PQRBANK	29-05-2007	PERSONAL LOAN	5,00,000
PQRBANK	22-05-2007	PERSONAL LOAN	50,000
ABCD BANK	09-05-2007	PERSONAL LOAN	5,00,000
PQRBANK	02-05-2007	AUTO LOAN (PERSONAL)	1,00,000
ABCDBANK	24-04-2007	CREDIT CARD	50,000
ABCD	21-09-2005	PERSONAL LOAN	2,40,000

Date of inquiry

Product of inquiry

Amount of inquiry

END OF CREDIT INFORMATION REPORT FOR RAMESH KUMAR

Disclaimer

All information contained in this credit report has been collated by Credit Information Bureau (India) Limited (CIBIL) based on information provided by its various members("Members"). Consequently, CIBIL does not accept any responsibility on accuracy, completeness, and veracity of any and all such information as provided. The information is current and up to date to such extent as provided by its members. Any information contained herein does not reflect the views of CIBIL or its directors or employees. The use of this report is governed by the terms and conditions of the Operating Rules for CIBIL and its Members.

Page 13 of 13

ANNEXURE-II

Sample Budgeting Sheet

Any budgeting exercise has four steps to it:

First Step : Prepare a monthly budget

Knowing your net monthly income and allocating specific amounts of money to each of your expense categories is the first step

Second Step : Capture actual expenses that you have incurred

To secure the correct outcome, it is important to capture actual expenses. It is recommended this activity be done on a daily basis so that none of the expenses gets missed out.

Third Step : Assess actual expenses against the budget

Keeping track of expenses being incurred against each of the categories is of high importance.

Fourth Step : Evaluate trend lines on your expenses

Evaluating the income and expense trends will enable you to gain insights on how you fare against the budget.

Step 1: Prepare a monthly budget

Income	Jan	Feb	Mar	Apr	May	Jun	Jul	Aug	Sep	Oct	Nov	Dec
Salaries												
Spouse												
Interest												
Other Sources												
Misc 1												
Misc 2												
Misc 3												
Total Income	0	0	0	0	0	0	0	0	0	0	0	0
Budget % of Income												
Budget in Rs	0	0	0	0	0	0	0	0	0	0	0	0

Budget Month	Rent	School Fee	Kitchen	Transport	Medical	Electricity	Telecom	Entertainment	Other 1	Other 2	Other 3	Other 4
Jan												
Feb												
Mar												
Apr												
May												
Jun												
Jul												
Aug												
Sep												
Oct												
Nov												
Dec												

- List all your incomes. In case of two earning members, please add both incomes while preparing budget
- Add any money that you can collect from other sources (such as bonus, incentive or even from selling of an old electronic item)
- This shall be your total money pool available for the month
- List all the heads under which you are expected to incur expenses such as rent/ child education/ kitchen/ electricity/ entertainment/ insurance premiums/ travel cost/ petrol or any other expense
- Add the loan EMIs or credit card outstanding that you are liable to pay
- Check on the excess of income over expense. In case the income is lower than the expense, you shall be required to revise your budget and reduce some of the expenses

Step 2: Capture actual expenses

Date	Select Category	Description	Amount
1-Jan-15	Rent		5,000
2-Jan-15	Kitchen	Grocery	2,000
5-Jan-15	School Fee	Avishka	3,000
5-Jan-15	School Fee	Amit	3,000
6-Jan-15	Transport	Petrol	1,000
8-Jan-15	Telecom	Mobile bill	1,000

- Capture date wise expenses against each of the categories
- Keep track of the actual budget and money spent against the budgeted amounts
- The endeavor has to be to restrict spending to less than the allocated money under a particular category

Step 3: Track actual expense against budget

	(ii)	(i)	(i)-(ii)
Budget Month	Budget Allocated	Planned Budget	Buffer In Budget
Jan	0	0	0
Feb	0	0	0
Mar	0	0	0
Apr	0	0	0
May	0	0	0
Jun	0	0	0
Jul	0	0	0
Aug	0	0	0
Sep	0	0	0
Oct	0	0	0
Nov	0	0	0
Dec	0	0	0
	0	0	0

- Tracking of actual expense against the budget shall help in taking corrective action if required

Step 4 : Evaluate trend lines on your expenses

Month	Rent	Kitchen	School Fee	Transport	Telecom	Others 1	Others 2	Others 3	Grand Total
Jan									
Feb									
Mar									
Apr									
May									
Jun									
Jul									
Aug									
Sep									
Oct									
Nov									
Dec									
Grand Total									

- Keep a track of your monthly expense trends. This shall help you to understand your needs better and shall also help you to fine tune your expenses
- A trend line helps you in future planning especially when you know (in advance) that in certain months your expenses tend to be higher for some reason (for instance a recurring lump sum expense like school fees for your child that needs to be paid in June and Oct). This will help you to plan your overall budgets for such months in a more organized fashion.

To download the soft copy for this budget sheet, please visit www.yourcreditscorebook.com

Recommendations

- Try to keep your expenses (including loan repayments to 80% of your net income)
- Allocate 10% of your savings to a contingency fund until it reaches a total equal to your 6 months of expenses
- In case you do not have term, health or home insurance, save a portion of your monthly savings to purchase such insurance covers
- If after the above steps you still have a surplus, utilize it to pay your outstanding in the following order of priority: credit cards, personal loans and then home loans.

ANNEXURE-III

The Credit Information Companies (Regulation) Act, 2005

Disclaimer: Text of this Act/Bill/Rules is abridged and is provided for informational purposes only. Please refer to the Gazette of India for the authentic text.

Credit Information Companies (Regulation) Act, 2005

A "Credit Information Company" as defined under the Act means a company formed and registered under the Companies Act, 1956 which collates and preserves records of an individual such as payments and dues pertaining to loans and credit cards among other credit information. The credit information company derives such details from respective banks and various credit institutions. These records help to curb the menace of the creation of Non–Performing Assets (NPAs) on account of bad debts, these records help the credit institution assess the credit worthiness of the individual and his capabilities to repay his debts and discharge his obligations in respect of the credit facility availed or being availed by him. These Companies have to ensure that such records are accurate. They can be penalized if they fail to do so.

The legislative intent behind the implementation of the Credit Information Companies (Regulation) Act, 2005 (**"CIC Act"**) was the need to provide support to the business of Credit Information. The act was promulgated to regulate the actions of credit information companies in India and to ensure the efficient distribution of credit and other such related matters.

The CIC Act is highly comprehensive and complex in nature. Pursuant to the CIC Act, the Reserve Bank of India and the Government of India have enacted the Credit Information Companies Regulations, 2006 (**"Regulations"**) and the Credit Information Companies Rules, 2006 (**"Rules"**) issued under the Act, respectively. The CIC Act, Regulations and Rules ("CIC laws") regulate the business of credit information

According to the CIC Act, every institution has to become a member of at least one Credit Information Company. (This now stands amended by the RBI notification dated 15 Jan 2015. As per the notification all credit institutions are mandated to become members of all CICs in India)

The CIC Act defines Credit Institutions to include the following:

i. a corresponding new bank, the State Bank of India, a subsidiary bank, a co-operative bank, the National Bank and regional rural bank;

ii. a non-banking financial company as defined under clause (f) of Section 45-I of the Reserve Bank of India Act, 1934

iii. a public financial institution as referred to in Section 4-A of the Companies Act, 1956

iv. the financial corporations established by a State under Section 3 of the State Financial Corporation Act, 1951

v. a housing finance institution referred to in clause (d) of Section 2 of the National Housing Bank Act, 1987

vi. a company engaged in the business of credit cards and other similar cards and companies dealing with distribution of credit in any other manner;

vii. any other institution which the Reserve Bank may specify, from time to time, for the purposes of this clause;

The CIC Act defines Specified Users as " any credit institution, credit information company being a member under subsection (3) of Section 15, and includes such other person or institution as may be specified by regulations made, from time to time, by the Reserve Bank for the purpose of obtaining credit information from a credit information company. The CIC Rules implemented in 2006 further broadened the scope of Specified Users and include the following institutions:

a) an insurance company as defined in the Insurance Act, 1938 and registered with the Insurance Regulatory and Development Authority;

b) a company providing cellular or phone services and registered with the Telecom Regulatory Authority of India;

c) a credit rating agency registered with the Securities and Exchange Board of India;

d) a stock broker as defined in the Securities and Exchange Board of India (Stock Brokers and Sub-Brokers) Regulations 1992 and registered under section 12 of the Securities and Exchange Board of India Act, 1992

e) a trading member registered with a recognized commodity exchange;

f) the Securities Exchange Board of India; and

g) the Insurance Regulatory and Development Authority.

Safeguards available to the Borrower under the Act

The term borrower is defined in section-2(b) as– "any person who has been granted loan or any other credit facility by a credit institution and includes a client of a credit of a credit institution; namely

i. a guarantor or a person who proposes to give guarantee or security for a borrower of a credit institution; or

ii. a person-

    a) who has obtained or seeks to obtain financial assistance from a credit institution, by way of loans, advances, hire purchase, leasing facility, letter of credit, guarantee facility, venture capital assistance or by way of credit cards or in any other form or manner; or

    b) who has raised or seeks to raise money by issue of security as defined in clause (h) of section 2 of the Securities Contracts (Regulation) Act, 1956 (42 of 1956), or by issue of commercial paper, depository receipt or any other instrument; or

    c) whose financial standing has been assessed or is proposed to be assessed by a credit institution or any other person or institution as may, by notification, be directed by the Reserve Bank;

The Act deals with the accuracy and security of credit information. While doing so the Act strives to adhere to maintain the privacy of the consumer. It is imperative that the Credit Information Companies and Credit Institutions provide data that is accurate, complete and duly processed and protected against any loss or unauthorized access or use, which shall be the responsibility of the Credit Information Company or Credit Institution. Section 20 of the Act elaborates on the privacy principles which shall be applicable to the credit information company, credit institution and the specified user. The principle has been made applicable for the purposes of processing, recording, preserving and protecting the information or data. The privacy of the consumer or the borrower is of prime importance and needs to be maintained by both CIC and its members. The privacy shall include the purpose of information, extent of obligation or any other information available during the complete process.

The credit information report is made available to the borrower on the payment of the requisite amount. This enables transparency in the system and enables the borrower to approach the right authority if there is any discrepancy in his report. The borrower may approach CIC or the credit institution or both for rectification, addition or deletion as the case may be. This however is subject to a dispute or error with regards to the credit information received by the borrower. Privacy and Security is the essence of the Act and that is evident from the fact that heavy penalty of Rs. 1 crore has been specified in sub-section (2) of Section 23 which may be imposed on the Credit Information Company, Credit Institution or any specified user for willfully failing to perform any act or engaging in any practice, in breach of the privacy principles under the CIC. The act mandates proper furnishing of documents to the relevant authorities and any deviation on this part may call for strict penalties. There can be no false transfer of information with regard to borrowers between Credit Information Companies. Individual penalties can be imposed on the officials of a Credit Information Company or other associated officials in their official capacity.

The Banking Regulations additionally provide for an alternate mechanism of the Banking Ombudsman to resolve the borrower's grievances. It must be noted that the Consumer Rights Act supersedes the CIC Act and if the borrower can also redress its grievance under the consumer protection act is in addition to any other remedy available in any other law for the time being in force.

Formation of Credit Information Company (CIC)

Every credit information company, in existence as of the commencement of the CIC Act shall apply in writing to the Reserve Bank for obtaining a certificate of registration under the CIC Act. To be able to commence the business of collating and preserving credit information, a certificate of registration is mandatory.

The RBI is vested with powers to cancel such certificates of Registration. The certificate can be cancelled if the company stops business or fails to comply with RBI conditions for registration or if the CIC fails to comply with Section 5 of the Credit Information Company and fails to submit books of account for inspection. RBI shall grant time to the company to comply with directions or condition of registration. However if the Reserve Bank is of the opinion that the delay in cancelling the certificate of registration of such company shall be prejudicial or detrimental to the public interest or banking policy or credit system or borrowers or other credit information companies, the Reserve Bank may cancel the certificate of registration without granting time. No order of cancellation of certificate of registration, granted to a credit information company, shall be made by the Reserve Bank unless such company has been given a reasonable opportunity of being heard.

A credit information company formed under the CIC Act is subject to regulations framed by the RBI in the prescribed manner. The CIC Act allows for the formation of multiple credit information companies subject to the provisions of the CIC Act. Generally, the powers of determining the number of credit information companies at any given time vests with the RBI which is subject to further review as required and the RBI also holds the power to cancel the registration upon satisfaction of certain conditions accorded in section 6.

Management of a Credit Information Company

The management of a credit information company should be assigned to a whole time chairperson and a part-time chairperson who can be of a non-executive nature. The Board of Directors should comprise persons having special knowledge in the fields of public administration, law, banking, finance, accountancy, management and Information Technology. RBI has powers under the CIC Act to supersede the Board under certain circumstances which shall affect the structure of the credit information company in a considerable manner.

Collection and furnishing of credit information

The Credit Information Company collects processes and collates information on trade, credit and financial standing of the borrowers of credit institutions which are members of the Credit Information Company. The CIC also provides credit scoring to its specified users or specified users of any credit information company or to other credit information company which is its member. Additionally the CIC undertakes any other form of business which the Reserve Bank may specify by regulations as a form of business in which it is lawful for a Credit Information Company to engage in.

A credit information company may require its members being credit institution or Credit Information Company, to furnish credit information as it may deem necessary in accordance with the provisions of the CIC Act within such period as may be specified in the notice. The Credit Information Company or specified User receiving credit information shall observe strict confidence and not disclose the information to any other person for any other purpose than as permitted or required by any other law for the time being in force.

Accuracy and Privacy Policies

Every credit information company, credit institution and specified user, shall adopt strict privacy principles in relation to collection, processing, collating, recording, preservation, secrecy, sharing and usage of credit information, as specified under the CIC Act. Every Credit Institution and Specified User shall adopt and comply with policies for processing, recording, preserving and protecting the data relating to credit information as specified by the Act. The CIC Act emphasizes on the need for accuracy of data stored by the Credit Information Companies and correspondingly lays down policies for allowing access to records containing credit information of borrowers and clients and alteration of records that needs to be adhered with.

Every credit institution shall, on receipt of request, furnish to the person a copy of the credit information subject to payment of such charges, as may be specified by regulations, by the RBI in this regard.

No credit information company shall refuse to register a credit institution or another credit information company as its member without providing reasonable opportunity of being heard to such credit institution or credit information company, whose application it proposes to reject and recording reasons for such rejection and a copy of such order of rejection shall be forwarded to the Reserve Bank.

Every specified user shall be entitled to obtain credit information for its use from the credit information company of which such specified user is a member.

Where a credit institution abstains from becoming a member or at any time is not a member of any credit information company, the Reserve Bank suo moto or on a complaint from credit Information Company may, direct such credit institution to take necessary steps within a stipulated time period to become a member of a credit information company. In case a credit institution fails to comply with the directions of the Reserve Bank to become member of at least one credit information company, the Reserve Bank may, without prejudice to the provisions of the CIC Act, intimate such failure to any other authority for taking such action as it may deem fit. (This now stands amended by the RBI notification dated 15 Jan 2015. As per the notification all credit institutions are mandated to become members of all CICs in India)

Powers of Reserve Bank of India as Vested in the Act

i. Power of RBI to supersede the Board of the CIC and appoint "Administrator":

   The RBI can to take over the management of the CIC for such period not exceeding six months, as may be specified in the order and which may be extended from time to time, however, not exceeding twelve months. Such supersession can take place when RBI is satisfied that it is necessary to do so in the public interest or in the interest of banking policy or credit system of the country, or for preventing the affairs of any credit information company being managed in a manner detrimental to the interest of banking policy or credit institutions or borrowers or clients or for securing the proper management of any credit information company. Additionally RBI may, on supersession of the board of a credit information company, appoint an Administrator for such period and on such salary and other terms and conditions as it may determine. The Reserve Bank may issue such directions to the Administrator as it may deem appropriate and the Administrator shall be bound to follow such directions.

ii. Power of Reserve Bank to determine policy:

   Where the RBI deems it necessary or expedient in the interest of the public or in the interest of the specified user or in the interest of CIC's or credit institutions or clients or borrowers so to do, it may determine the policy in relation to functioning of credit information companies or credit institutions or specified users generally or in particular and when the policy has been so determined all credit information companies, credit institutions and specified users, as the case may be, shall be bound to follow the policy as so determined.

iii. Power of Reserve Bank to give directions:

   RBI is authorized to issue directions in the following matters

   - In the public interest or in the interest of Credit Institutions or in the interest of specified users or in the interest of banking policy or to prevent the affairs of any CIC from being conducted in a detrimental manner or to secure proper management of CIC
   - Require the CIC to call a meeting
   - Depute one or more of its officers to observe the meeting.
   - Appoint officers to observe the affairs of the CIC
   - Direct the CIC to make changes to its management, etc.
   - The RBI can either on a representation or on its own volition cancel or modify any direction issued by it to a CIC.

iv. Inspection of credit information company, credit institution and specified user: The Reserve Bank, at any time, may on being directed so to do by the Central Government shall, cause an inspection to be made, by one or more of its officers or through such other persons or agency as the Reserve Bank may determine, of any Credit information company or credit institution or specified user and their books and accounts. A copy of its report on such inspection and the Reserve Bank shall be supplied to the credit information company or credit institution or specified user, as the case may be.

v. Power of Reserve Bank to make regulations: The Reserve Bank may make regulations consistent with the provisions of the Act and the rules made there under to carry out the purposes of the Act.

Functions of Credit Information Companies

A credit information company may engage in any one or more of the following forms of business, namely:

- Collect, process and collate information on trade, credit and financial standing of the borrowers
- Provide information to specified users or to the same of any other CIC
- Provide credit scoring to its specified users or to the same of any other CIC
- Undertake research project
- Undertake any other form of business on the discretion of the RBI

Settlement of Dispute

As far as dispute settlement, when there is no remedy available under the CIC Act, on matters related to credit information, the matter shall be resolved by using the Arbitration and Conciliation Act, 1996. The arbitrator should be appointed by RBI and the matter has to be resolved by the arbitrator within three months. Provided that the arbitrator may, after recording the reasons therefore, extend the period up to a maximum period of 6 (six months). Provided further that, in an appropriate case or cases, the Reserve Bank may, if it considers necessary to do so (reasons to be recorded in writing), direct the Parties to appoint an arbitrator in accordance with the provisions of the Arbitration and Conciliation Act, 1996 for settlement of their dispute in accordance with the provisions of that Act.

Offences and Penalties

The Act lays down offences and penalties for offences. For the purpose of deciding the penalty the RBI shall serve notice on CIC or Credit Institution or Specified User, as the case may be, requiring it to show cause as to why the amount mentioned in the notice should not be imposed as penalty and a reasonable opportunity of being heard shall also be given. No complaint shall be filed against CIC or Credit Institution or Specified User, in any court of law in respect of any contravention or default in respect of which any penalty has been imposed by the RBI in accordance with the CIC Act. Any penalty imposed by the RBI under the CIC Act shall be payable within a period of 14 days from the date on which notice issued by the RBI on the CIC or Credit Institution or Specified User and in the event the said institution fails to pay the sum within such period it may be imposed on a direction made by the principal civil court having jurisdiction in the area where the registered office of the CIC or Credit Institution or Specified User, being a company, is situated and in case of credit institution incorporated outside India, where its principal place of business in India is situated.

Glossary

Active Credit Accounts A customer's loan or credit card accounts which are currently active

Asset Valuables owned by an individual including property, cash or any other investments

Bankruptcy A legal declaration given by a person stating his inability to repay his debts. In India, this is enforced through a court of law

Borrower Individual taking a loan or credit facility from a lender

Budget Financial plan for a definite period of time with an objective of tracking income and expenses

CIBIL Credit Information Bureau Of India Limited. CIBIL is one among four bureaus in India

CIBIL TransUnion Score Credit score generated by CIBIL

CIC Credit Information Companies Act - 2005. This Act details the functions and responsibilities related to data management by a credit bureau (CIC) and its members (credit institutions). This Act also outlines the rights of consumers (individuals whose data is reported by members)

Co-borrower Joint applicant of a loan. A joint applicant bears the same obligation to repay the loan as a borrower

Code of conduct for Collection Companies A code laid down by IBA (Indian Banking Association) to be followed by each bank in the process of collecting dues from a delinquent customer

Collateral Property or any other asset that is offered to the lender(by a borrower) as a security against the loan amount

Collection Process of approaching borrowers to collect the overdue amount on their loan facilities

Collector Individual working on behalf of lending institutions for the collection process

Credit Buying or borrowing in the present and repaying in parts over the future

Credit Bureau A data repository which collects and distributes data pertaining to consumers and rates them on associated risk for various lending products

Credit bureau flags Flags depict the status of a credit facility - settled, write off, post write off settled are a few examples of negative flags

Credit Error An incorrect update on a credit bureau is called a credit error

Credit Health This term defines the state of credit well-being of an individual

Credit History Detailed record of a borrower's various credit facilities and repayments on them over time

Credit Inquiries A request by any lender for credit history of a consumer as recorded on a credit bureau

Credit Limit Maximum amount fixed by a bank as the limit on an individual's credit card utilization

Credit Monitoring Monitoring of credit activity by an individual so as to be able to track changes in his credit profile, detect suspicious activity and prevent identity fraud

Credit Repair A process that helps to restore, enhance and protect a person's credit profile

Credit Report A comprehensive compilation of a person's credit history

Credit Score A score based on the historical data of a borrower. This score signifies the risk associated with a borrower and is used by underwriters to assess credit risk

Creditor Financial institution/ individual who has extended a credit facility

Crif Highmark One among four credit bureaus in India

Cybercrime Cybercrimes are criminal activities carried out using a computer and the internet

Debt Burden Ratio A formula used to calculate the repayment capacity of an individual.

Debt Consolidation Merging all existing loans into one loan is termed as debt consolidation

Default A situation of non-payment of loan or any other credit facility is termed as default

DPD Acronym of "days past due". Refers to the number of days a credit account is overdue

EMI EMI (Equated Monthly Installment) is the fixed amount that a borrower needs to pay towards his term loan on a pre-defined date of every month

Equifax Multinational credit bureau headquartered in Atlanta, USA. Equifax is one among four credit bureaus in India

Experian Multinational credit bureau headquartered in Dublin, Ireland. Experian is one among four bureaus in India

Guarantor A person who undertakes to repay a loan in the event of default by the borrower

Home Loan A loan which is used to buy a residential property

Identity Theft Identity Theft is a financial fraud where an individual's name and papers are used by a fraudster for a financial gain.

Insurance Insurance is a process of "making good the losses" in the event of pre-specified damages, illness or death in return for payment of a specified premium

KYC "Know Your Customer" refers to the validation of the identity of consumer by collecting approved and valid documents. The documents to be collected under KYC are Identity Proof and Address Proof

Lending Institution Financial institution which provides credit facilities (such as banks, NBFCs)

Lien A right to keep possession of property belonging to another person until a debt owed by that person is discharged

Loan A legal agreement between a borrower and lender where the lender gives funds and borrower agrees to pay as per agreed terms

Major Credit Errors The errors on a credit report which affect the credit scores negatively are called major credit errors

Masked(undisclosed) Report A credit report which does not disclose important information like "Name of Lending institution" and "Account Number". This report is usually provided by the bureaus to a lending institution which has inquired on an individual (with a bureau)

MasterCard A financial service provider which provides payment technology to banks and credit card companies across the globe

Minimum amount due Least amount of money required to be paid by a borrower to keep his account in current status

Minor Credit Errors The errors on a credit report which do not impact the credit score of an individual are called minor credit errors.

NBFC – Non Banking Financial Company A company registered under the Companies Act, 1956 and approved by the RBI to act as a financial institution

Personal Loan A cash loan given to an individual based on the profile of the borrower and without any security

RBI "Reserve Bank Of India" is the central bank of our country. It is an autonomous body that decides on the functioning of the banks and any other financial institution

Retail Lending All loans or any credit facility offered to an individual is termed as retail credit

Revolving Credit Revolving credit is a type of credit facility which does not have a fixed tenure of repayment (such as a credit card)

Settlement With reference to a credit facility, a settlement is an official agreement between creditor and debtor to resolve over dues (usually by offering a waiver on the total outstanding)

Social Score Score derived by judging an individual's credit character based on his activity on social platforms such as Facebook and LinkedIn

Subprime Borrowers Borrowers with a poor credit profile

Term Credit A credit facility extended for a fixed period of time

Trade line Any credit account or credit facility reflecting in a bureau report

TransUnion Multinational credit bureau headquartered in Chicago, USA. This bureau operates in India through a collaboration with CIBIL

Underwriting The process of decision making (on any loan application) by a lending institution

Verification agency An agency appointed by a lending institution to check the authenticity of information furnished by an applicant

Visa card A financial service provider which provides payment technology to banks and credit card companies across the globe

www.freescoreindia.com A portal which provides the credit report and score to consumers free of cost along with a detailed analysis of the report

Write-off Term used in a credit report when a lender declares the overdue amount to be non-recoverable

Disclaimer

This book, "Unlock the Power of your Credit Score" ("Book"), is presented solely for informational purposes so that the reader is assisted in his goal to be credit healthy. The information contained in the Book, should not be in any way, construed to offer any professional advice, including advice, in relation to any legal, accounting, tax and financial purposes. Any references made in this Book are only for informational purposes, from data available in the public domain, so as to better analyse and illustrate the concepts and strategies contained in the Book. While best efforts have been used in preparing this Book, the authors make no representations or warranties of any kind and assume no liabilities of any kind with respect to the accuracy, correctness or completeness of the contents of the Book and specifically disclaim any implied warranties of merchantability or fitness of use for a particular purpose. The authors shall not be held liable or responsible to any person or entity with respect to any loss or incidental or consequential damages caused, or alleged to have been caused, directly or indirectly, by the information contained herein. Every reader is different and the advice and strategies contained herein may not be suitable for a particular reader. The readers are advised to seek the services of a competent professional before commencing upon a credit health management or an allied program.

About the Authors

Arun Ramamurthy

Arun Ramamurthy is a management graduate from IIM Calcutta and holds a bachelor's degree in Economics from Presidency College, Calcutta.

Arun has had a long and distinguished career in Indian retail banking with various multinational banks. Arun has been at the forefront of the retail lending industry in India. In his role as business head, he was instrumental in setting up and running large teams.

An avid reader, fitness enthusiast and entrepreneur, Arun seeks to spread financial knowledge for the betterment of our society at large.

Gaurav Wadhwani

Gaurav Wadhwani is a management graduate from MDI Gurgaon. Gaurav is a seasoned banking professional with over a decade of experience. He specializes in the fields of credit, credit policy and credit analytics.

Gaurav is a firm believer of the fact that the interests of borrowers and lenders are co-terminus. Both borrower and lender need each other not only for meeting personal and business objectives but also for the overall benefit of our economy.

Aman Kapoor

Aman is a literature graduate from Delhi University and is a seasoned retail banker. Aman has worked with various multinational banks and has had extensive exposure to credit markets in India and abroad.

Aman's vision is to have a Credit Healthy India where every individual has equal opportunity to access the credit markets.

****Arun and Gaurav are co-founders of Credit Sudhaar; India's leading Credit Health Management Company. Credit Sudhaar is an online platform which helps clients to manage their credit profiles and save money.**